The Past Masters

A ~~Cass Canfield~~ BOOK

Lloyd George and Churchill: the greatest of them all

Harold Macmillan

The Past Masters

Politics and Politicians

1906–1939

HARPER & ROW, PUBLISHERS

New York, Hagerstown, San Francisco, London

FIRST U.S. EDITION

ISBN: 0–06–012814–3

LIBRARY OF CONGRESS CATALOG CARD NUMBER: 75–29880

76 77 78 79 80 10 9 8 7 6 5 4 3 2 1

Contents

List of Illustrations

List of Illustrations

Daniel Macmillan and his birthplace

CHAPTER ONE

An Honourable Ambition

THE heroic, the dominating, figure in my childhood – all the more romantic because his life and death were so long ago – was that of my grandfather, Daniel Macmillan. Although he had died in 1857 and I did not enter this world until nearly forty years later, he seemed to me almost a living person; for we were brought up as children upon the story of his struggles and achievements. I still have in my room a picture of the little stone croft, now ruined, on the Cock of Arran, in which he was born.

Although there is nothing unusual in the experiences of a poor Scots boy coming south in his teens to found a business in London, yet there was something remarkable about my grandfather quite unrelated to his commercial success (which was, at any rate in his lifetime, of a very modest kind). What remained for his descendants was the short but beautifully drawn picture of a man of unusual charm and character which was written by his friend Tom Hughes, the author of *Tom Brown's Schooldays*. This little book I read and re-read in my early childhood, and it had a great effect upon me. I was determined somehow to follow in his footsteps by my own will and effort. Whether this would be in the field of art, literature or commerce, I did not know for sure. But, if I remember aright, by the time that I had started to go to a little day-school in London I had already made up my mind that the most probable and attractive arena for my efforts would be in the world of politics.

There was one passage in Hughes's biography of my grandfather which particularly appealed to me. In 1833, when he was a young man of twenty, his restless ambition was reproved by his elder brother Malcolm, now a schoolmaster in Stirling. He replied as follows:

You seem rather to like twitting me about being ambitious, and this is the third or fourth time you have said, 'What are you, or your father's house, that you should be ambitious?' I have once or twice thought of giving you an answer. I shall do so now. You must not think me angry though I speak warmly. I have too much respect for you to speak disrespectfully. So you must not mistake me.

What am I? A very humble person who had no objection to raise himself if he could do it honourably. If all my relations were slaves, I should not feel that I was bound therefore to be a slave, that is, if I could purchase my freedom. I do not feel bound to follow in the footsteps of any of my relations. I am here to act for myself. None of them can stand in my stead in any very important matter. The most important things must be done by myself – alone.

He goes on to describe his upbringing, after a reference to his brother's question, 'What is my father's house?'

Well, to begin with father; though I was very young, only ten, when he died, I have the deepest reverence for him. He was a hard-working man, a most devout man, and as I have heard mother say, cared for nothing but his family, that is, did not care what toil he endured for their sakes.

This is not a bad description of my own father, especially as regards his devotion to his family. He goes on:

You knew him better than I did, you can value him more highly. I now remember with pleasure, and with something better than pleasure, the manner in which he conducted family worship. Though I did not understand a word of his prayer, the very act of bowing down on my knees did me good, at least I think so.

He continues in the same strain:

Of my mother I can speak what I do know. I know her as well as ever a son knew a parent, and my persuasion is that she is the most perfect lady in all Scotland. With so little knowledge derived from books, with so very little intercourse with the higher ranks of society, with so little care or thought on what is most pleasing in external conduct, was there ever a lady who, so instinctively, so naturally, did what was

The author at twelve

right, acted with so much propriety in all cases? She has such high
and noble notions that no one ever heard her say, or knew her do, a
mean thing, no one could ever venture to say an impudent thing to her,
or talk scandal in her presence. If any one did so once, it never was
repeated; some quietly spoken but most bitter and biting saying put an
end to such garbage.

If my grandfather had been ambitious, I would be ambitious too.

Of course there was a short period, during the Boer War, when
the fame of great soldiers inspired our imaginations. I had wit-
nessed, on the afternoon of 19 May 1900, the vast crowds gathering
round Hyde Park Corner to pay homage to Lady Baden-Powell,
the wife of the gallant defender of Mafeking. I had sported, like
my comrades at the day-school where I attended, noble portraits
of Lord Roberts and Lord Kitchener in my buttonhole. But this
mood soon passed. We were not a military family, and my parents

had few army or navy officers among their friends. There was, of course, Colonel St Aubyn who lived next door; but his only interest for me was as father of two adorable daughters, for both of whom I had a deep and impartial affection. But if the fighting services were remote from our lives, literature and politics were matters of daily discussion. Moreover, there was a special connection, at least in one field of political and social problems, which flowed from my earliest memories. For there was a lively tradition in the family regarding such matters which had its roots in my grandfather Daniel's early beliefs. Next to that of Daniel, the two most respected names in our household were those of Frederick Denison Maurice and Charles Kingsley. Naturally I had not read Maurice's famous *Kingdom of Christ* as a child, although I have read it since and admired it deeply. But Kingsley was dear to us for many reasons; above all we loved that splendid romance *Westward Ho!* and *The Water Babies*, one of the best books for children ever written. Engraved portraits of these men hung in my father's library. I saw them every day. Under the influence of Maurice and Kingsley my grandfather had become a devoted adherent of a small, but influential group which was to become known as the Christian Socialist Movement. It began about the time of the Chartist agitation and the World Revolutionary Movement of 1848. It was, in a sense, a precursor of the Fabians, although it was fundamentally religious rather than political. In reality it had developed no economic doctrine. It was a social movement based upon an intense feeling for the poor and the suffering. It was applied Christianity. Of the later developments of this genuine effort for reform on Christian lines I need not speak. It took many forms, of which the foundation of the Working Men's College was the most tangible result. Meanwhile the fundamental radicalism – the desire for reform – continued to inspire many men and women, and formed a part of our own heritage. A cynic might say that as the family became more prosperous it became more prudent. However the spirit remained; and for that reason my father and his nearest relations were brought up in the tradition of Liberalism in its broadest sense. It was only when

Charles Kingsley   *Frederick Denison Maurice*

Mr Gladstone, by his conversion to Home Rule for Ireland in 1886, broke the Liberal Party that they found themselves entering upon new connections. They became Liberal Unionists, giving their support to the eighty or so dissident Members of Parliament who followed Lord Hartington and Joseph Chamberlain.

Yet, in spite of the schism of 1886, the most respected name in my childhood was that of Mr Gladstone – the G.O.M., or Grand Old Man. There were signed pictures of him – a whole row of informal photographs – in the spare bedroom. There were stories of his friendship – or at least acquaintance – with my great-uncle Alexander, who lived to continue and expand Daniel's work.

There was the famous occasion when his praise of Stribling, my great-uncle's coachman, sent that loyal retainer into ecstasies of joy. For, in spite of it all, Gladstone (certainly after Disraeli's death) dominated British politics and overtopped, like a great peak, all his rivals. Yet if Mr Gladstone represented the dedicated politician, ready to devote his long life to incessant labour in the service of the state, he was by no means a solitary figure in this respect.

It has recently become the fashion to denigrate everything and everybody – and naturally politicians are an easy butt for every critic, in the Press or on the air. Certainly, in my youth, they were not chary of attacking each other. Perhaps the rapier was more common than the bludgeon. At any rate, the 'cut and thrust of debate' was a reality, not a mere phrase. The reports of Parliamentary discussions and of the occasional speeches of leading statesmen at public meetings were voluminous – and read with avidity by the somewhat limited electorate of those days. But whatever the politicians might occasionally do to ridicule one another, they were held in high esteem by the public. For this, there were many reasons. Members of Parliament were unpaid; and somehow the public always likes amateurs. The great majority of Members had no desire for office. They sat, often unopposed, in Parliament after Parliament, for constituencies which had elected their fathers and grandfathers. Many, of course, were the eldest sons of peers. Parliamentary sessions normally began in February and ended half-way through August – as they still do in the United States, Australia and other democratic countries. An autumn session was practically unknown. So Parliament did not interfere unduly with normal country life. Grouse, partridges, pheasants had been disposed of, a reasonable amount of hunting had been managed, before the call of the Parliamentary Whips. Only, perhaps, the keen fisherman could complain.

At the same time the leading lights were few – and these protagonists held a dominating position on a less crowded stage. The making of money had not yet become so necessary or so absorbing – and in any case a successful banker or merchant of

Gladstone speaking near Snowdon

good repute could hold a seat with general respect, without finding it necessary to inflict parliamentary questions or speeches upon his colleagues in order to please his constituents. Finally, the long tradition of the country, which through the struggles of centuries had raised this small island to be the head of a great empire, accustomed to play a major role in world affairs, was a powerful inspiration for young and aspiring minds. Fame was still the spur. Nor did the break-up of the Liberal Party in 1886 make any difference in the character of Parliament. Ambitious and eager men from the universities, from the professions (especially from the bar), and from a larger class than can be easily remembered today men living on their means, sometimes considerable, sometimes modest – came forward with enthusiasm in support of the great parties. If some old friendships were broken over Ireland, the tradition of Parliamentary courtesy and social friendship remained. Nevertheless, the combination of the Conservatives and the Liberal Unionists – seceders from Gladstone – was the dominant power of my childhood. The Unionist Government, which had lasted almost twenty years, was not overthrown till the election of 1906. By 1910, apart from the Irish vote and the new Labour Members, the Unionists had recovered equality with the Liberals.

It is perhaps worth recalling for the benefit of those whose knowledge of recent history is limited that it was this adhesion of support from the very core of Liberalism which had such a profound effect upon the Conservative Party and its fortunes. I remember, when I was leader of the party, being reproved by a deputation of the 1922 Committee in these words, 'You don't seem to remember, Prime Minister, that this is a Conservative Government.' To this I replied, 'But the last purely Conservative Government was formed by Mr Disraeli in 1874.' I went on to say: 'The Liberal Unionists kept Lord Salisbury and the Conservatives in office for twenty years and the Liberal Unionist Party did not finally merge with the Unionists or Conservatives until just before the First War. Even today it is the twenty or thirty Liberal Nationals who help to keep us in power. Moreover it is the fact that we have attracted moderate people of Liberal tradition

Sir John Simon   *Ernest Brown*

and thought into our ranks which makes it possible to maintain a Conservative Government today. A successful party of the Right must continue to recruit its strength from the Centre, and even from the Left Centre. Once it begins to shrink into itself like a snail it will be doomed.' Incidentally, the Liberal Nationals included some outstanding Parliamentarians, of which perhaps the most notable was Sir John Simon. Another was Ernest Brown, a very engaging character, a former sergeant-major gifted with a stentorian voice. He became Minister of Labour in one of Mr Baldwin's Governments. It was said that the Prime Minister, who used a neighbouring room, complained of the noise. 'What's Brown doing,' he asked, 'to make all that row?' 'He's speaking to Edinburgh,' was the reply. 'Why doesn't he use the telephone?'

Naturally I knew but little of these grave questions as a child. Yet I have a vivid recollection of listening to conversations on similar topics amongst my elders and betters in the last years of the nineteenth and the opening years of the twentieth century. My father, although temperamentally a man averse from any form of public commitment, retained his broad outlook on affairs. He sympathised and supported my mother, who threw herself with enthusiasm into the Liberal Unionist organisation. I can well remember troops of ladies coming into our house in London for what I suppose were committee meetings. Large and overwhelming they appeared to me when I peered at them through the banisters – with their huge hats, feather boas and furs. They formed no doubt the controlling authority in the Women's Liberal Unionist Association. Of this my mother was either honorary treasurer or secretary.

Thus by the time that I was beginning to take an interest in public affairs there were three streams which irrigated the virgin soil of my young mind. First, the old radicalism of the Christian Socialist Movement. Second, the orthodox Liberalism which my family supported until the Home Rule split. Third, the Unionist, but definitely not Conservative or Tory forces, which united in a strange partnership the most respected of the Whigs, Lord Hartington, and the great radical reformer, Joseph Chamberlain, who preferred to range himself behind a Conservative Administration rather than allow what he regarded as the threatened break-up of the Empire. At any rate, by the time I had been a year or two at my preparatory school, my mind was made up. My grandfather had been ambitious, and proud of it. I would follow – and try to emulate his achievements. What should by my sphere? I was the youngest of three brothers. My eldest brother (eight years my senior) was already distinguishing himself in scholarship. I knew that my second brother's dearest hope was to go to the bar. I would go into the House of Commons.

Later on, from the age of twelve onwards (that is to say after we had settled in Sussex) I was fortunate in being able during the holidays to observe and listen to some of these men of whom one could read in the newspapers or hear others speak. The General Election of 1906 took place in January of that year. We were in London for Christmas and shared the mild and protracted excitement of that contest; for in those days elections stretched over a period of three weeks or more. We used to stand outside Harrods to see the inspiring spectacle of effigies of Balfour and Campbell-Bannerman climbing up their respective ladders as the results were announced day by day. Not unnaturally, since by then my father and mother were keen Balfourians, I tended to favour Campbell-Bannerman. In other words I was reverting to orthodox Liberalism.

In Sussex our nearest neighbour was Lord Robert Cecil. He represented then a form of High Toryism, sternly attached to old traditions in Church and State. I can never forget the firmness and even violence with which he argued, or the extraordinary charm with which he treated boys and youths as worthy of serious discussion. Two issues especially excited him in those pre-war days. He felt strongly about the Marconi case (where Lloyd George and other Ministers were eventually acquitted of anything worse than lack of judgment). He was passionate about the threat to the Established Church in Wales. But he was just as keen on golf and lawn tennis, at both of which games he displayed unexpected ingenuity and cunning. His style on the putting green was remarkable. He stooped almost to the ground and, holding his putter at the bottom of the shaft, holed his ball from incredible distances. At lawn tennis he had a devastating shot (learned from real tennis) with a great deal of cut on the ball. This could be very dangerous on the grass courts of those days. The First War came as a terrible shock to Lord Robert and seemed to alter his whole outlook on life. While retaining his charm and social qualities, he seemed now obsessed by the horrors of war and the dangers of militarism. Deeply religious, careless of everything but his one theme, he spent all the years of his life from 1920 onwards in a crusade for the League of Nations and the principle of collective security. He became a non-party, or rather an all-party man. He laboured long and, alas, unprofitably. For the instrument to which he trusted was first gravely weakened by American defection and then shattered partly by weak and partly by evil men. Nevertheless, his tall, stooping figure with its great head and prominent nose lives in my memory – and that of many others – half Savonarola, half Don Quixote, respected by all, loved by many, and adored by little children. (He could waggle his ears, and did so, on request, for their delight.)

Very different, in spirit and temperament was John Morley, an old friend of the family and of the firm – he had been for many years Macmillans' chief literary adviser. Morley represented what might be called the old radicalism. As strongly anti-Socialist as he was anti-clerical, he retained the traditions of Cobden and Bright and the intellectualism of J. S. Mill. He was a charming, delightful, if rather prim, and even old-maidish character. But he was wonderful in conversation, whether literary or political. I cannot refrain from quoting his very generous tribute, at the end of his life, to my great-uncle, Alexander Macmillan.

The great publisher is a sort of Minister of Letters, and is not to be without the qualities of a statesman . . . The head of the house of Macmillan [Alexander Macmillan] had these qualities in the full sense and measure proper to his task . . . He went about his work with active conscience and high standards. He had the blessing, both attractive and useful, of imagination, added to shrewd sense and zeal for the best workmanship. His eye for the various movements in his time of knowledge and thought, literary, scientific, and religious showed extraordinarily acute insight. He knew his world: it comprised the most enlightened of the divers social strata, and he gathered a body of men around him with many vigorous talents, with his own strict exaction in way of competency, and his own honourable sense of public responsibility.

Among other neighbours were some notable Liberals. James Bryce (later Lord Bryce) historian, statesman and diplomat – he proved one of the most successful of British Ambassadors in Washington. We respected his learning, but his conversation seemed often rather obscure. Then there was Herbert Paul, now living in retirement, the brilliant editor of the *Daily News*, who, if he had not been struck down by illness, might have played a considerable role in Parliament. On the other side there would

John Morley
from a drawing by Sandys

Lord Robert Cecil

sometimes come Miss Balfour, Arthur Balfour's sister, a close friend of my mother. I remember seeing Balfour at our London house, but only for a few moments. Very impudently I asked for and obtained his photograph.

What dim figures these must seem to people today! Yet they were highly characteristic of the powerful groups of men who, ranged on either the Conservative or Liberal side – long before the rise of the Labour Party – dominated the political scene. They were drawn from what I suppose would now be called the 'governing class' or the 'establishment'; partly from the nobility and gentry and partly from men of intellect who had raised themselves by their efforts, chiefly in scholarship and learning, to prominent positions. It should be remembered that apart from any question of the powers of the House of Lords, peers played a great part in the governments of those days, continuing the system which had operated throughout the eighteenth and nineteenth centuries. Even after the defection of an important section of the Whig nobility, Mr Gladstone's last Government of 1892 contained five peers, including Lord Kimberley as Secretary of State for India, Lord Rosebery as Foreign Secretary, Lord Ripon as Colonial Secretary and Lord Spencer as First Lord of the Admiralty. For some fourteen years the Prime Minister, Lord Salisbury, was in the House of Lords, and for a great part of that time held in addition the post of Foreign Secretary. Even the Liberal Government of 1905 which swept their opponents out of power and place in a 'democratic' flood, contained five peers, with the Admiralty, the Board of Agriculture and the Colonial Office entrusted to noble hands. Mr Bonar Law's Government, formed seventeen years later, after the fall of the Lloyd George coalition, actually had eight peers out of a Cabinet of seventeen.

It will be seen, therefore, that there was no division but rather an amalgamation of power at the top both in politics and in social life. The great Liberal and Conservative hostesses still held their sway and men took their place, from whatever origin they were sprung, according to the merits of their intelligence and achievements. At the same time there was a very close association between politicians and men of literary and artistic distinction, as well as with leaders of finance and commerce. Looking back, perhaps with the normal tendency of old age to exaggerate the virtues of the great men remembered from my youth, they seem in my eyes so far from dim, much more firmly sculptured figures than those who now fill the public eye.

On the Tory side Balfour, even after his fall from the leadership of the Conservative Party in 1911, remained a unique personality. Descended from the mixed blood of a successful Scottish merchant and a long-established aristocratic family, he had no doubt been aided in the beginning of his career by being Lord Salisbury's nephew. But his predominance was due to the rare mixture of highly trained intelligence (he was no mean philosopher and author of philosophic writings), with quite remarkable charm. Beneath that gentle and courteous exterior one sensed an iron strength of will – his rule in Ireland in the bad

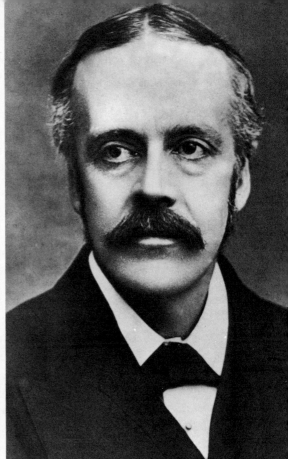

H. H. Asquith   *A. J. Balfour*

times proved his quality – but in ordinary company he seemed still something of a Prince Charming.

Equal to Balfour in Parliamentary skill, Asquith stood out supreme among the Liberals. He had made his own way in the world, from modest origins, by sheer force of brain power and application, passing from scholarship to scholarship, winning university prizes, achieving an outstanding position at the bar and finally succeeding without question after Campbell-Bannerman's death in 1908 to the leadership of the Liberal Party and the premiership. It used to be said that Asquith looked like a Roman senator. He also talked and thought in a perfect classical style. If Balliol at this time prided itself on an 'air of effortless superiority', Asquith was pure Balliol. But his very gifts were perhaps a weakness – certainly in war. For he presided over a Cabinet like a great judge. He did not lead it, as Chatham did (and later Lloyd George and Churchill were to do) like a supreme commander. I only met Asquith once in those early years. His youngest son – by his first wife – Cyril (or Cys) was a year or two senior to me at Oxford, but I came to know him well. Like all his brothers he was a brilliant scholar. He won all the honours and all the university prizes in the true Asquithian manner. On one occasion (I think in 1913) he invited me to stay for a night or two at No. 10. Most of the family were away, but the Prime Minister gave us dinner and two or three hours of his company before going to bed. I think this happened on two successive nights. I cannot recall the conversation, except that it was scholarly (with many classical references) and taut. You could not risk either banalities or insincerities.

Bryce and Morley were more men of thought than of action. Few perhaps read their books today, but they are well worth reading. Many other politicians, on both sides, including of course Balfour himself, were respected as authors and thinkers.

Though we did not know it, we were approaching the end of an era – the period when Britain reached perhaps the apogee of her strength and influence: unchallenged and unchallengeable. My childhood covered its last years – from 1897, Queen Victoria's second jubilee, till Armistice Day 1918. A generation later, from 1939 to 1945, there was to be our last and splendid act, 'our finest hour'. Then the curtain was to fall on the mighty imperial drama.

All these influences gave to my childhood and youth, before I went to Oxford, a background where politics were keenly felt and discussed, sometimes with deep emotion, but always with good manners. It was in these years that I picked up by chance a copy of *Sybil*. From that I was led to read Disraeli's masterpiece *Coningsby*. Then there were published, in 1910 and 1912 respectively, the first two volumes of one of the greatest biographies in our language, the life of Disraeli by Monypenny and Buckle. These fascinated me; and somehow throwing aside all the other more staid and decorous statesmen whom I would see or about whom I would hear, I became entranced by Disraeli's romantic

Mr and Mrs Asquith ; Cyril Asquith inset

career. If Dizzy had made himself leader of a party and Prime Minister by his own unaided effort, could not I have a go? Moreover, from Disraeli I learnt that *laissez-faire* and Free Trade were not dogmas, but at the best expedients. Things could be done, and must be done, above all in the social field.

Meanwhile there had arisen in the Liberal Government before the First War a new and strange phenomenon – Lloyd George. Compared with him, Balfour, Asquith and all the rest seemed cast in another, and a traditional, mould. They followed the old, well-trodden paths. Lloyd George was different – and so too, in his own way, was Churchill. They would be lost in calm weather; like petrels they would revel in wind and storm.

It should be remembered that General Elections were very different from today not merely in the manner by which they operated but in the character of the electorate. The third Reform Bill, that of 1885, had extended the franchise chiefly to add the agricultural workers, then about one million, to those of what were then called 'the working classes', enfranchised by Disraeli's Reform Bill of 1867. Nevertheless since there was no women's vote and the conditions upon which a man could obtain a vote were quite stringent (he had to be a householder with a year's residence in one place), there was no question of an automatic vote for every person above twenty-one, let alone eighteen. The actual electorate was limited to just over a quarter (27 per cent) of the adult population. There were in addition some 500,000 'plural votes'. Many of the smaller boroughs did not have more than a few thousand electors. I can remember attending public meetings before the First War when it was a common practice for the chairman, before calling upon a candidate to answer a question or in reproving a heckler, to use the phrase, 'Are you a voter, sir?' Nine times out of ten he was not. There was no question of these enormous bodies of voters with which the modern candidate has to struggle, sometimes rising to eighty or one hundred thousand. Moreover, with few telephones and no motor cars, campaigning was a more leisurely affair. A large number of constituencies returned their Members unopposed –

Electioneering in 1910

it was almost thought rather bad form to contest a constituency where the result was obvious and the Member had been long installed. For instance in the 1900 General Election, 243 out of 670 Members were returned without a contest. By a strictly guarded convention peers did not take part in electoral contests. At the same time the fact that there was neither radio nor television gave much greater weight to the speeches of the leading figures which were printed, often in full, in the Press. These took up almost as much space as was devoted to a romantic murder or a titillating action for divorce, which were in those days reported blow by blow. It was in these great electoral contests, two held in the single year – 1910 – that Lloyd George made his reputation as the greatest platform speaker of the day, rivalling even Gladstone's Midlothian tours. Many reviled him as a demagogue; none could ignore his growing power and influence.

Before passing to some memories of this extraordinary man – the most dominating figure of my youth and early manhood, it would perhaps be appropriate to say something of the old House of Commons, both as I remember it in my youth and in my first years as a Member. I have referred to the absence of radio and television, thus making the platform and the hustings the dominating power in General Elections. To this must be added the importance of debates in Parliament. The serious Press gave many columns to an account of the major debates in both Houses, unlike the meagre reports of today. The speeches of statesmen made in various provincial towns, often following each other in restating their own and refuting their opponents' cases, were given equal prominence. At the same time there had grown up and was about to develop with its full strength the power of the popular Press, whether of editors or proprietors. Lord Northcliffe, with his *Daily Mail* and *Evening News* and afterwards by his purchase of *The Times*, controlled something of the order of two-thirds of the metropolitan Press. Later Lord Beaverbrook began to push the *Daily Express* into rivalry. People may find it difficult to understand today how these magnates exercised so much political influence. The answer is simple. Without the radio and television

Lord Northcliffe   *Lord Beaverbrook*

the Press had the monopoly of news and views. In the seventeenth and eighteenth centuries, and to some extent in the nineteenth, the pulpit was a powerful weapon of propaganda. But this gradually passed to the Press whether serious or popular. Among the editors, perhaps the most notable was C. P. Scott of the *Manchester Guardian*. Statesmen in the war and post-war years, however much they might dislike them, could not altogether ignore the tastes or fancies of the Press Lords. Now that the monopoly is broken and power has passed into other hands, politicians have to learn to face the 'box', and the trivialities of the commentator have taken the place of the more ponderous judgments of the leading article. But in the course of this transformation statesmen have, perhaps, lost a little of their dignity, and certainly of the 'mystique' which once surrounded the commanding personalities.

CHAPTER TWO

Lloyd George

I

IT would be wrong to draw the conclusion from these sketches of the political figures of my childhood and youth that the years in which I grew to manhood were ones of quiet or decorous procedure unaccompanied by bitter controversy. On the contrary, in many ways debates were more acute and more violently conducted both in Parliament and in the country. This was partly because the subjects under discussion were ones about which every one without technical knowledge could form an opinion. War in South Africa; Home Rule for Ireland; Welsh disestablishment; Dreadnoughts for the Navy; religious or secular education; attacks on landlords and the House of Lords – all these were unlike the dreary subject of 'economics' with its vast apparatus of statistics and its stultifying jargon, which leave most of us lost in a jungle of confusion. In those days the electors were free voters and not enslaved by the pundits. We could all have our own view. All these were matters upon which the opinion of the man in the street was as good as that of the expert. Moreover, they were the kind of matters which had been fought over for two or three centuries. They were familiar and correspondingly enjoyable, in spite of the violence and the perils.

Into this scene, and gradually dominating the stage, there was projected one of the most remarkable men who have ever entered into the tempestuous arena of politics – David Lloyd George. No doubt today he is almost forgotten by the general public, so

Lloyd George at the beginning of his career

short is their memory of politicians. Yet by the end of the first quarter of the century, he was the outstanding public character in Britain and indeed in Europe.

He began, at the age of twenty-seven, by his election as Member for Caernarvon by a majority of eighteen. He was to hold it for fifty-five years, until his acceptance of a peerage in 1945, a few months before his death. Unlike other leading statesmen – Gladstone, Balfour, Asquith, Churchill, Bonar Law – he never had to undergo the bitterness of losing his seat. When his family – son, daughter and son-in-law – eventually joined him as Welsh Members, his support became strengthened locally, even when weakened nationally. Meanwhile, from 1890 till 1905, he was an independent, rebellious, often truculent 'back-bencher', almost more feared by his friends than by his opponents. He teased Mr Gladstone by demanding Welsh disestablishment and Home Rule for Wales. With the change of government in 1895 and the approach of the Boer War, he became the leading, and by far the most effective, critic of the policy into which Joseph Chamberlain led his somewhat reluctant colleagues. Yet he probably caused more anxiety and distress to the Liberal 'establishment' – the Liberal Imperialists, as they were called – who gave general support to the Government's policy. These men – Lord Rosebery, Asquith, Haldane, Grey – were the élite of the Liberals. They were also the products either of long Whig and Liberal tradition or of university and bar. Lloyd George, who boldly declared that all these ideas were obsolete and that the day of 'the cottage boy' had at last dawned, took the opposite view. He opposed the war, publicly and violently, in the House and on the hustings. He opposed its origin and purpose; he also denounced its 'barbarous' conduct. Campbell-Bannerman was the only one of the Liberal establishment who had any sympathy for him. Campbell-Bannerman had to try to steer the party, of which he was elected leader, on some middle course. The question naturally occurs even to the most superficial student of this period. How did this little Welsh solicitor, without money, without influence, an orphan brought up by his old Uncle Richard, the shoemaker of Llanystumdwy, without friends among, or much sympathy with, the leading Liberal politicians, who adopted throughout the whole South African War so extreme a position of bitter criticism as to endanger his personal safety and to lead to such extraordinary scenes as the famous Birmingham riots in December 1901, when he had to escape through the back of the Town Hall disguised as a policeman; who attacked in violent and abusive language not only the Church of England in Wales but the personalities of its Bishops – how did this man, by his own unaided efforts, and often fighting both against the tide of public opinion and the attitude of his official leaders – how did such a man achieve in these fifteen years of opposition such a position in Parliament and the country that when at last, after nearly twenty years in the wilderness, the Liberals returned to power in 1905, he was offered the important post of President of the Board of Trade, and became three years later, on Asquith's succession to the premiership, the only possible and undisputed claimant to the great position of Chancellor of the Exchequer who lodged in No. 11 Downing Street, and was the neighbour and often heir apparent to the occupant of No. 10?

The answer lies in the power of this new man who had arisen from the people to speak to the people and for the people in novel but thrilling tones. He was, in a sense, the true successor to Joseph Chamberlain, the radical reformer. Yet Chamberlain, like Bright and Cobden, was a middle-class employer, who held and developed radical views and policies. All the same, he was in modern parlance (so penetrated are we today with Marxist terminology) unmistakably and ineradicably 'bourgeois'. Lloyd George, though of long ancestry of which he was proud, and, no doubt, like all Celts, descended from great kings or heroes, was a man of the people. He had moreover qualities of charm far greater than Chamberlain. Lloyd George could follow a virulent attack, in the language of pure demagogy, by a passage of simple and moving appeal, in the language of pure poetry. It was this combination of qualities that made him, all through his life, at once so attractive and so formidable. He could blow you out of the water with a broadside of vilification; the next moment you were rescued, soothed, captivated into helpless surrender. It used to be said of him later that 'he could charm a bird off a tree'. It was this which made him so successful in bringing settlements in several dangerous industrial disputes, both in the railways and in the mines. But his strength lay in the fact that he was not a mere actor. Both moods were sincere. He could love and hate – and sometimes both at once. Of course, he liked a scrap – a good row – both in his young days and in his old age. But he was ready to take as well as give; and, of course, he generally gave as good as he got.

At the Board of Trade he was studiously moderate, in his most conciliating mood. 'There has grown up a new Lloyd George,' wrote *The Times*. 'The new, but ever courteous Minister . . . bitterness has gone from him,' said the *Daily Mail*. He carried successfully a number of useful measures – a Merchant Shipping Bill, a new Company Bill, an Employers' Liability Insurance Bill and a new Patents Bill, at the protectionist flavour of which some Liberals raised their eyebrows but which correspondingly won Conservative approval. The reform of the Consular Service and some useful agreements with France, Belgium and Switzerland to allow trade samples to clear the Customs without delay pleased the commercial classes. There was only one row, and that was not too serious. In a speech criticising the House of Lords for throwing out some important Liberal Bills, he used the phrase 'If an Election has to come,' he declared, 'it will come on the issue of whether this country is to be governed by King and peers or by the King and his people.' This was deeply resented by King Edward VII and a painful correspondence followed between Buckingham Palace and Downing Street. But it was only the first ranging shot. The great barrage was to follow.

1909 was the year of Lloyd George's first Budget, soon to be known as 'The People's Budget'. In modern terms, the sums involved seem modest. He had to provide for the Old Age Pensions – the first national pension scheme in our history was passed in 1908. He had also to meet a heavy demand for naval construction. In the course of the Pensions Bill he let slip a phrase which became

Lloyd George in 1908 with Megan

*Megan Lloyd George
and the People's Budget, 1909*

famous – and a gift to cartoonists. 'I have no nest eggs. I am looking for someone's hen-roost to rob next year.' But the 'robbing' was on a very small scale. Income tax was raised from 1*s.* to 1*s.* 2*d.* and a super-tax (as it was then called) of 6*d.* was imposed on all incomes over £5,000. A rise in death duties (then moderate enough), a small increase on spirits and tobacco – that was all the immediate addition. But coupled with this was the famous scheme for Land Taxes, intended primarily to tax an 'unearned increment'. This, the first of several attempts (all fruitless) in the last half-century or more, caused a violent storm. The attack was not on developers (as they have come to be called) but on landlords. A bitter contest followed, which altered political history and was to lead, in due course, to virtual 'single-chamber government'. In fact, the

Finance Bill, which was ill-drawn and very complicated, had been so amended as to prove almost unworkable. If the Tory leaders had been wise, they would have been satisfied by this achievement in Committee stage. But they were not wise – they were led (greatly to Lloyd George's delight and relief) to throw out the Bill in the House of Lords. This produced another famous phrase. A Conservative Member had rashly praised the House of Lords as 'watchdog of the Constitution'. The retort was memorable. 'You mean it is Mr Balfour's poodle.'

In the long conflict which followed Lloyd George played a leading role. There were two General Elections in 1910, and although in the United Kingdom the Liberal and Conservatives were practically equal on both occasions, the Government could rely on the support of the forty odd Labour Members and the Irish contingent of eighty. For this, of course, a price had to be paid. For the former it was modest, £400 a year Parliamentary salary. For the latter, it was of vast implications – Home Rule for Ireland. In this long-drawn-out campaign Lloyd George distinguished himself by the vitality and violence of his attack. Asquith, emulating Pericles, delivered sonorous passages of limpid eloquence. Lloyd George, like Cleon, let them have it. At Limehouse, he went for the Dukes, especially of Northumberland and Westminster, with their leaseholds of ever-increasing value. At Newcastle, it was Dukes again; fully equipped Dukes cost as much to keep up as two Dreadnoughts: they were just as great a terror and they lasted longer. At Wolverhampton there was a general attack on the hereditary principle. 'They have no qualification – at least they need not have any. They do not have to have a medical certificate . . . they only require a certificate of birth – just to prove they are the first of the litter. You would not choose a spaniel on these principles.' All this sounds very small beer now. But sixty years or more ago it was quite exciting – and, from a Chancellor of the Exchequer, unusual.

But Lloyd George was not merely an agitator. He was a builder. With Old Age Pensions and National Insurance he opened up a new era. Many people, of all parties, had studied the problem of

The Oxford Union: Gilbert Talbot, first back row; Austen Chamberlain, second middle row; Macmillan, second front row

poverty. Lloyd George did something about it. He can indeed claim to be the founder of the Welfare State. Whether he would have approved all its developments is hard to say. For he believed, like all men of peasant stock, in hard toil, self-respect and self-reliance.

The restriction of the Lords' veto powers to a delay of two years led inevitably to a crisis in the summer of 1914. For then the Home Rule Bill would pass into law and the clash would come. At first, many Liberals treated the threat of Ulster resistance as bluff. But as the months passed, the danger grew. At last, following something like a mutiny in the Army, we seemed in July 1914 to be drifting towards the cataract. But, by the bullet of an assassin at Sarajevo, a tragic stream of events was set in motion which brought us not to civil war in Ireland but to the First World War.

During this period the most exciting event in my undergraduate life at Oxford was Lloyd George's visit to the Union Society. He was invited by Gilbert Talbot, a strong Conservative, when he was President in the summer of 1913. After much cajoling, he agreed. It is difficult to imagine the effect of this visit on the University and City of this tremendous, dynamic figure. We were accustomed to imbibe Liberal doctrine through the classical periods of an Asquith, a Simon or a Herbert Samuel. The fierce radicalism of our great Welsh orator was something new, with bitter memories of 1909 and the Limehouse and Newcastle speeches. It was as if a Cleon or a Danton had suddenly invaded our quiet academic groves. I well remember the scene – the great force of police, the vast crowd of Town and Gown, the anxious Proctors – all the show. In the event, the great man 'came, saw and conquered'. I recall most vividly his wonderful performance – the rapid changes from grave to gay – from slow to quick – now menacing, now seductive. I can still see the tremendous head, with the long raven-black hair. I did not see him again for many years. When at last I saw him at a distance, from the Strangers' Gallery of the House of Commons after the war, the noble head was there – more deeply lined – the great shock of hair was as white as snow.

Yet during these pre-war years, now scarcely remembered, Lloyd George's efforts were by no means confined to social reform and class warfare. He was a sincere patriot and was quick to see the growing German menace. It was on his own suggestion that in the middle of the Agadir crisis, in the summer of 1911, he used the occasion of the annual bankers' dinner in the City of London to deliver a stern warning to the Kaiser and the German Government. He had, of course, agreed the passage with the Foreign Secretary (Grey) and the Prime Minister (Asquith). Coming from the Chancellor of the Exchequer, whose whole life and record had placed him almost among the devoted pacifists, its significance was unmistakable. 'If a situation were to be forced upon us in which peace could only be preserved by the surrender of the great and beneficent position Britain has won by centuries of heroism and achievement, by allowing Britain to be treated, where her interests were vitally concerned, as if she were of no account in the Cabinet of Nations, then I say emphatically that peace at that price would be a humiliation intolerable for a great country. like ours to endure.' The Kaiser and his naval advisers knew what these words meant. The German gunboat *Panther* did not stay long anchored off the Moroccan port of Agadir.

Behind the scenes, unknown to the general public, Lloyd George had larger plans in mind. He wished now to calm the internal storm in order to face the external hurricane that seemed, to many well-informed observers, to be blowing up. For the Germans, having lost Bismarck, had never found a successor. They were small men, dominated by able but narrow military cliques. Accordingly, after the death of King Edward VII in May 1910, he worked hard, with the help of Churchill and F. E. Smith, with much sympathy from Balfour, to bring about a 'National Government' with an agreed programme. Already, in the previous year, he had discussed such a plan in some detail with some of his intimate friends. Apart from some compromise on Home Rule, which might involve 'devolution' both in Wales and Scotland, an agreed plan of social reform, an impartial enquiry on tariffs (Lloyd George was never a hidebound or fanatical Free Trader) the most exciting suggestion was a system of National Service. This ambitious plan almost succeeded. It was not Balfour, or even his leading associates, who blocked the path. It was, as always in politics, the small, mean-minded characters who are known as 'good party men'. On the Liberal side there would, of course, have been similar objectors. But this 'grand design' hardly known at the time might perhaps have averted the Great War. At any rate, we should have started off with a million trained reservists. To Lloyd George and to him alone, the credit is due, and great was his disappointment when this last opportunity was missed.

Then followed some harassing years. The so-called 'Marconi scandal' (in which he was accused of corruption in league with Rufus Isaacs, the Attorney-General, his brother Godfrey Isaacs, and Lord Elibank, the Chief Whip) ended in acquittal of any charge more serious than folly and bad judgment. But a whole year – from April 1912 to June 1913 – was taken up with a flow

'Mr Lloyd George and his Guardians' by Max Beerbohm

(*Though he was Chancellor, Lloyd George was thought so innocent in money matters that C. F. G. Masterman and Sir Rufus Isaacs had to coach him on his evidence to the Marconi Committee.*)

of libel, scandalous charges and innuendo – and to no purpose, even of financial gain. Ministers were formally acquitted; but their reputations were tarnished. They had been shown as stupid and thoughtless; and that is almost as bad for politicians as being proved wicked.

Even the Land Campaigns, which he launched in 1913, did not make much impact. The urban population were bored, the rural sceptical. His great attack on game and sport fell flat, largely because he relied on a phenomenon which no one had ever seen – a field of mangold-wurzels utterly destroyed by pheasants. He never heard the last of this gaffe. At the Oxford Union debate, mangold-wurzels were thrown about in the debating hall. Alas, pheasants were out of season.

While my friends and I spent the happy weeks of the Trinity term of 1914 in the beauty of unspoilt Oxford enjoying a glorious summer, events moved on inexorably till the fatal day. On 4 August, for Lloyd George too, the whole first phase of his life was ended. He was fifty-one. He was to serve eight more years, six as Prime Minister, in conditions of difficulty and danger hitherto unequalled in our history. On 22 October 1922, as the result of a revolt within the Conservative Party the Coalition was broken up. Lloyd George, after seventeen continuous years in office, fell from power never to return.

II

In the course of eight tremendous years – 1914 to 1922 – Lloyd
George rose to a pinnacle of fame unequalled by any man since
Chatham and only to be rivalled in the next generation by Churchill.
He demonstrated his superb qualities as an administrator by his
achievement in the creation of the Ministry of Munitions. He
has described how he began his task. He was given some rooms in
Richmond Gardens (Disraeli's old house), a secretary, a deal table,
and two Windsor chairs. Within a few months he created a strong,
virile and powerful department. For this alone he will be remembered as the man who saved the Army from the confusion
and incompetence with which the provision of armaments of all
kinds had been handled by the War Office. With his large vision
he multiplied by many times the official demands of the services,
whose chiefs seemed quite incapable of realising the huge needs
for guns, shells and machine-guns which would be necessary to
fight the war in its new form. The embattled fortresses, stretching
for hundreds of miles from Switzerland to the North Sea could
only be assaulted by an unparalleled expenditure of artillery fire.
Nor could modern infantry hope to defend or attack a position
without lavish use of the machine-guns. The distinguished cavalry
officers who were to command through the whole war the finest
body of infantry ever put into the field were beginning to learn
their lesson. But Lloyd George was far ahead of them. For his
purpose he created, by a typical British compromise, an organisation which combined civil servants and business men, aided by
representative local organisations, and became an instrument
which rapidly brought into service all the plant and labour already
available with huge additions of unskilled labour, women and new
machinery, some Government owned, some Government sub-
sidised. When I was at the Ministry of Supply in the Second War,
all we had to do was to revive, with some modifications and
adaptations to changing service demands, the machine which
Lloyd George had constructed.

When he became Prime Minister at the end of 1916 there was a

Machine-gunners on the Somme

universal feeling that he was 'the right man in the right place'. Whatever might be the rights and wrongs of his struggle with the military authorities, any generous student of those years must agree that he was surrounded with immense difficulties. It is true that he never achieved the same influence on strategy or the same co-ordination of the services as his great successor Churchill. He could not prevent the horrors of the campaigns of the Somme – when Asquith was still Prime Minister, or of Passchendaele in his own time. Nevertheless he had a right to claim that he was the greatest War Minister in our history, and he was properly acclaimed as the architect of victory. In any case, such a vast literature exists about the conduct of the war in all its aspects, that I should not attempt to add to it, all the more because I have no personal memories to contribute. For the first two years of the war I was an active soldier, mostly in France. On the Somme (September 1916) I received my third and decisive wound and spent the next period, till the Armistice (November 1918), mainly in hospital. I saw little of my old friends (for I was in very poor shape) and no leading politicians. I remember that when the news of Asquith's fall came to us (in December 1916) I felt sorry for the old states-man but relieved that we should at last have some drive and energy at the top.

After the war, in the spring of 1919, I went for a year to Canada. By the time I returned I sensed that Lloyd George's position, although still powerful, was beginning to be undermined. But I saw little and learned little of the inner history, for I was now married and hard at work learning a new profession in the family publishing business.

Certainly the years that followed the end of the war (1918 to 1922) were troubled, inconclusive and in many respects dis-appointing. Yet it is unfair to blame upon Lloyd George all the faults of the Treaty of Versailles. So far as the territorial settlement of that Treaty was concerned there was little to complain of; and if the attempt to demand excessive reparation from Germany was later to become apparent, yet Lloyd George was one of the first to try to mitigate the excessive claims. At a series of con-ferences he struggled hard to this end. The last, and most dramatic, the Genoa meeting, failed; and with it collapsed the hopes of moderate men for a revival of Europe. All through this period he was frustrated by what seemed French intransigence. For the French, having failed to obtain the security which Marshal Foch believed could only be achieved by holding the Rhine frontier, and having seen the American retreat into 'isolation', were deter-mined at least to keep Germany down and prevent a new German threat. As so often in history, Allied policy fell between two stools. 'Enemies,' wrote Machiavelli, 'should either be annihilated or conciliated.' We achieved neither of these objectives. *Hinc illae lacrimae.* In any event, Lloyd George at least achieved, again

Passchendaele

with difficulty and after a fierce struggle against French opposition, the delivery of food supplies in the early months of 1919, to save the German people from starvation. Keynes has left a dramatic record, unhappily not so well known as his famous attack in *The Economic Consequences of the Peace*, which describes this strange story. After several months of inconclusive discussion among officials, Lloyd George determined to bring the matter to an issue. The Council of Four had not yet been created, and the whole body of 'Allied and Associated Powers' were represented at a huge meeting, with fifty to sixty delegates. There was general agreement that food must be sent. German ships could be made available. The food was all ready. But who should pay for it? The Germans proposed to pay in gold. The French Minister of Finance, M. Klotz, objected. For, although the sum was only £5 million, yet by this payment the total resources of Germany available for reparations would be correspondingly reduced. In the debate which followed, Lloyd George used every weapon in his rhetorical armoury. He declared that the honour of the Allies was at stake. Moreover the British troops would not tolerate the sight of starving women and children in the occupied areas. A telegram from General Plumer (now in command of the British Forces) was brought in (by pre-arrangement) and read out with immense effect. As for M. Klotz, clamouring for his 'gold', Lloyd George, with a few gestures, represented him as another Shylock. He would do more to Bolshevise Germany than Lenin or Trotsky. Clemenceau knew that he was beaten and after a few efforts to save his Minister's face, gave in to all the British Prime Minister's demands. Clemenceau is said to have remarked afterwards, 'Poor me! There is only one stupid Jew in France, and he is my Minister of Finance.' Nor should it be forgotten that in spite of the so-called 'Carthaginian Peace', in fact Germany never really paid any reparations to the Western world which were not covered, and more than covered, by the sums which she borrowed from America and on which she ultimately defaulted. If Lloyd George could have had his way the impossibility of any large transfer of wealth from one country to another except by way of goods and services would have been

Lloyd George and Clemenceau   *M. Klotz*

recognised at an earlier date and thus Hitler would have been deprived of his grievance and his propaganda for revenge.

Nor should the story of Ireland be forgotten. It was due to his efforts, supported by Churchill and Birkenhead, that the Treaty was signed which seemed to bring to an end, after so many centuries, the Curse of Cromwell. It is true that in Ireland there is never a final end to the old struggles. But the Irish Treaty brought at least fifty years of peace; and the friendship between the Governments of London and Dublin, even with the new troubles in Ulster, remains unbroken, if sometimes strained.

Why then did the prestige of the Coalition begin to decline about 1920, until its final collapse in 1922? Why was Lloyd George destined to leave office at the age of fifty-nine, never to return to power? In the first place, he had made many mistakes and many enemies. As often happens, at the summit of his career, hailed as the greatest man in Britain and perhaps in Europe, he became vain and egocentric. He treated some of his chief colleagues

not only cavalierly but often rudely. Curzon and Milner felt this
bitterly. He tried to manage everything and seemed to grasp more
and more authority into his own hands. His personal staff – known
as 'The Garden Suburb' – with its enlarged size and functions,
became offensive to the established departments, such as the
Treasury and especially the Foreign Office. Secondly, with his
continual absence at a series of conferences, he neglected the
House of Commons. His huge nominal majority became a danger,
with intrigue and dissatisfaction rampant. Thirdly, the resignation
of Bonar Law, the leader of the Conservative Party, in the spring
of 1921, on grounds of ill-health, was a final blow. For it was this
strange partnership between two men so different in character
and temperament which kept the balance in Parliament. Bonar
Law would warn Lloyd George against some of his extravagant
notions and imaginative, but often impracticable, plans. But
Bonar Law always supported his chief, when trouble came, with
determined, grim and unshakable loyalty. When Austen Chamberlain, an agreeable and high-minded, but weak, man succeeded,
things began to go badly wrong. Fourthly, it must be admitted
that the 'honours scandal' did Lloyd George great harm. Of course,
everyone knew that for many generations contributions to party
funds from rich supporters, Conservative and Liberal, had in due
course been rewarded by baronetcies and peerages. But there was
a decent veil over these transactions and the recipients were almost
always men who had given long service to the party and were
held in general respect. Under the Coalition the system degenerated
into something like an open sale. Nor were the recipients beyond
reproach – indeed in one or two cases they were men of low repute.
The King protested in many instances, but in vain. Moreover,
while in pre-war days the party funds were established and
accepted for what they were, there was a mystery about the
Lloyd George fund which was never satisfactorily explained and
which haunted him for the rest of his life. He claimed that these
contributions were given to him to be used at his discretion in the
national interest. He certainly used the money partly to support
the Liberal Party (when it was temporarily reunited) and partly

With the Prince of Wales

to finance the splendid series of investigations which he instituted between the wars and which were of real importance and value. All the same, in 1920 to 1922 the Lloyd George fund was a source of malignant innuendo and ribald jokes. It was something different from the old system of party funds. If those did not always smell too sweet, this one positively stank.

Finally, after all the trials of four years of war and four years of uneasy peace, the nation was exhausted. It wanted to forget about the distracting foreign complications and concentrate on domestic issues, now, with declining trade and rising unemployment, becoming more and more compelling. Above all, no more military adventures. Thus the danger of a new war against Atatürk, the rising power in Turkey which suddenly seemed to loom before a distracted people, was the last straw. Actually, by a most successful diplomacy from London and a brilliant conduct of a delicate situation at Chanak by General Sir Charles Harington, peace and honour were saved. But the public had suffered a fright.

All these factors contributed to Lloyd George's fall. But underneath them all lay the change in the national mood. Bonar Law fought the General Election on the cry 'Tranquillity'. Lloyd George dismissed it with a contemptuous phrase, 'It is not a policy, but a yawn!' Yet it was just what the people wanted.

The Liberal Party was deeply split on the fall of Asquith in 1916, and although the numbers that followed Lloyd George for the war were somewhat larger than those who were true to Asquith, yet the official party machine slipped out of Lloyd George's hands. The Liberal tradition was offended by his new methods and ambitions. Moreover, the most distinguished members of the old Asquith Cabinet refused to serve in the new Coalition, and Lloyd George was forced to rely on Conservative statesmen or independents. He thus began to seem to the true Liberal a deserter and even a traitor.

The General Election of 1918 – characterised by Asquith as 'the coupon election' – increased the bitterness between the two groups. For those Liberals who had supported the Government through all its trials were given the blessing both of Lloyd George

Andrew Bonar Law as Prime Minister

and Bonar Law. They stood as 'National Liberals' and generally obtained local Conservative support. The official Liberals (who, in Asquith's words, stood 'without prefix or suffix') controlled what remained of the Liberal machine. 133 of the former and only 28 of the latter were returned, although they polled about the same number of votes. The Conservatives swept the board with, altogether, the Government claiming over 478 supporters, out of 707 seats. Since the 73 Sinn Fein members refused to take their seats, the Government's position was on paper overwhelmingly strong.

Yet by the near elimination of the old Liberal Party (even Asquith lost his seat) Lloyd George's own position was really made more precarious. He was now, in a sense, the prisoner of the Conservatives. As long as Bonar Law remained, the Coalition held, for Bonar Law held the Conservative Party to any course which seemed good to him. It is remarkable that when he returned to politics in 1922, he resumed his authority and by his speech at the party meeting persuaded the majority, against the advice of their leader, Austen Chamberlain, to break up the alliance. The next day Lloyd George resigned.

Since I never met Bonar Law, I cannot add anything of value

to the official accounts of his life and accomplishments. Lord Blake has written an admirable biography under the rather harsh title of *The Unknown Prime Minister*. Elected leader of the party, after Balfour's resignation, as a compromise candidate (his rivals were Austen Chamberlain and Walter Long), he never rose to supreme office until he was too weakened by ill-health to prove his worth. But throughout the war and the immediate post-war years he was a perfect second-in-command. A dour Scot, of Lowland origin, with roots both in Ulster and Nova Scotia, he was the exact opposite to that mercurial Celt, Lloyd George. He was trusted by his party, who followed him with absolute loyalty. Taciturn, sceptical, pessimistic – he was the perfect foil to Lloyd George.

It was only after long hesitations that he decided to return to politics in 1922. He had kept his seat, but had been on a long holiday in the South of France. He was no doubt largely influenced by Lord Beaverbrook who admired and loved him.

He became Prime Minister at the end of 1922. Before the spring had passed into summer, a fatal cancer caused his resignation and death. He had suffered greatly from the war, in which he lost two sons, and from the death of his wife. Perhaps his spirit, as well as his body, was broken. But he was a true patriot.

Meanwhile Lloyd George was left without any firm base. At the General Election of 1922, only 62 of his followers were returned. Although the official Liberals only numbered 54, the tradition and sentiment of the party followed Asquith. At the General Election of 1923, when the issue was Free Trade or Protection, the two wings entered into an electoral alliance, and gained 159 seats. But the Labour Party, with 191, were now ahead, and were called upon to form a Government, although enjoying no majority. But the Liberal reunion was only skin deep. For the next decade and more they were divided, partly by old memories and partly by the new and adventurous policies which Lloyd George began to advocate. By 1935 the Liberals had split into three groups; the official Liberals (under Sir Herbert Samuel), the Liberal Nationals (under Sir John Simon), each numbering just over twenty, and Lloyd George's family party of four.

Megan Lloyd George canvassing in 1910   *Violet Bonham Carter canvassing in 1921*

During all this time the feud was kept alive largely by family loyalties; Violet Bonham Carter (Asquith's daughter) and Megan Lloyd George were the redoubtable antagonists who would never allow the hatchet to be buried. There were occasional attempts to patch things up, usually just before a General Election. But the two groups soon fell apart again. I remember a story about one of these efforts which Gwilym Lloyd George, a dear friend for many years, once told me. His father used to go through with him any speech he was to make. On this occasion he intended to say, 'I don't know why Sir Herbert Samuel has such a grudge against me. I have never done him any injury. After all, I made him the first Procurator of Judaea since Pontius Pilate.' (He had appointed Samuel Governor of Palestine under the Mandate.) Gwilym protested – 'But, father, this is supposed to be a meeting to reunite the Liberal Party. You can't say that.' 'Oh, yes, I will. It's jolly good, and I mean to say it.' After an hour's argument, he persuaded his father to refrain. Many years later, when the old man was near his end, he took his son's hand, who was sitting at his bedside, and thanked him for all the years of loyalty and filial devotion. He added, his eyes creasing up into that wonderful smile which many still remember, 'I've only one thing against you. I wish you'd let me say that about Herbert Samuel.'

Looking back, it is clear that after the Liberal schism events followed on an inevitable course. The Coalition fell apart; the Conservatives consolidated their position and formed a party Government under Bonar Law, and later Baldwin. The Liberals by their internal strife and weakness laid the foundations for 'the rise of the Labour Party. Liberalism therefore lost its position as a party of the Left and Left Centre based upon a historic position going back for more than a century. Conservatism was able to strengthen itself and develop along new and broader lines. The Liberals lost to the Right and to the Left, and ended up in a position of weakness from which they have never recovered.

I had been introduced to Lloyd George at Oxford in 1913. I did not meet him again until 1924, when I entered Parliament for the first time. He was still by far the most romantic figure in the House. He was the best parliamentary debater of his, or perhaps any, day. Churchill's speeches were powerful but prepared in his own style, where every word was written out beforehand. Impressive as they might be, they lacked flexibility. This was particularly true when he no longer spoke from the Front Bench after 1929 and he had not the use of the 'Box' on which to place his text. Lloyd George who spoke from few notes commanded batteries as powerful as Churchill's but much more mobile. Not being tied to a text he could adapt and change with a remarkable rapidity, and pick up a point from an interruption like lightning. For instance, when a young Conservative member jeered at Liberal dissensions with the witticism 'in the Liberal Party there are many mansions', Lloyd George called out, like a flash 'and in the Conservative Party there are many flats'. I have only two or three times heard him on the platform, where he was equally if not more effective. In 1924 he still held the rapt attention of Members,

Lloyd George, Lord Reading, Sir Herbert Samuel

who flocked in when his name came up on the 'ticker' in the various rooms. In spite of the disadvantage of not speaking at the end or beginning of a debate – this was reserved for the Government and the official Opposition – and speaking from his corner on the third bench below the gangway on the Opposition side, he overcame this tactical disadvantage. He devised a very skilful technique, which he later explained to me.

I first got to know him in a peculiar way. In my rather hesitating, shy and stilted style I delivered a speech (not my maiden speech, but in the early years of the Parliament) to which by chance he happened to listen. As usual the House was very thin for new Members, especially Members on the Government side who were only called at times when the audience was small. Into my speech I put all the thought and care that I commanded. It was on an economic subject, dealing with unemployment and its possible cures. I had worked hard at it and it was received with respect. Later in the evening Lloyd George came up to me and said, 'Macmillan, that was an interesting speech of yours.' I was naturally flattered. He continued: 'If you don't mind my saying so, you

have no idea how to make a speech.' I answered, 'Will you tell
me?' and with great kindness he took me up to his room to give
me his fatherly advice. It ran something like this. 'First of all you
are a new Member. You always speak in a thin House, probably
in the dinner-hour. Even I am not called till six. Never say more
than one thing. Yours was an essay, a good essay, but with a large
number of separate points. Just say one thing; when you are a
Minister two things, and when you are a Prime Minister winding
up a debate, perhaps three. Remember your own position. There
will be few listeners. What you want is that somebody will go
to the Smoking Room and say, "You know Macmillan made a
very good speech." "What did he say?" someone will ask. It must
be easy to give a ready answer – one point. Of course you wrap it
up in different ways. You say it over and over again with different
emphasis and different illustrations. You say it forcefully, regret-
fully, even perhaps threateningly; but it is a single clear point.
That begins to make your reputation.'

Then he went on to explain that my speech had been delivered
in a monotonous way without light or shade. 'What is the right
way?' I asked. 'Why, there must be continual variation; slow
solemn phrases, quick, witty amusing passages. Above all say to
yourself as you get up, "Vary the pace and vary the pitch." This is
the heart of the whole matter. Finally, don't forget the value of
the "pause".' I have never forgotten his advice and watched him
over and over again with admiration. He would start generally in a
low tone, and knowing that he had to give time for Members to
come into the Chamber from the Dining Room or the Smoking
Room, or the Library, his opening sentences were of a vague and
introductory character (just as in the opening few minutes of a West
End play). I remember his explaining this to me in some detail.
'You can't have the murder in the first few minutes because the
stalls and so on are still coming in. The butler comes on; the
telephone rings; the soubrette comes on, and after five or ten
minutes when the audience are settled down the play begins.'

When I protested, 'But how do you do this?' he replied, 'Oh,
it's quite easy. The speaker who has just sat down in a thin House

Lloyd George the orator

is probably a serious but not exhilarating speaker. You say that you have listened to his speech with the greatest interest and sympathy. There is just one point you didn't understand. Why did he say that there is no difference between black and white? He rises to explain. You courteously give way. When he sits down, if the House has filled up, you accept his explanation with a suitable apology. If not, you say that of course you now understand, but still, why did he say that there is no difference between green and yellow? He rises, a little angrily. You give way. The little comedy is repeated. Then, your audience having arrived, you start your speech.'

I have seen him use this method many times. In addition to his histrionic powers, he had a beautiful voice, rather high-pitched, and the hands of an actor. In moving his arms or hands he could describe a whole scene and bring it to life.

My friendship – I can almost call it that – with Lloyd George continued to develop during the 1924 to 1929 Parliament. He took occasion to come into the Chamber when I spoke on economic or industrial subjects, and showed his warm approval. He liked the little book – *Industry and the State* – which some of my friends published in 1927. My co-authors were Oliver Stanley, Bob Boothby and John Loder. I even ventured to invite him to a little dinner in one of the small dining rooms to meet them and other sympathisers, who formed a sort of 'progressive Tory group', afterwards christened the Y.M.C.A. I took the precaution of asking his secretary what he would like. His tastes were very simple: chicken (not game, which perhaps reminded him of landlords) and a little Irish whiskey and water. He was a marvellous guest, for he was a grand listener. He drew us all out and seemed really interested in what we had to say. When the evening was over we felt rather ashamed. He should have been the talker, and we the listeners. But he delighted in young people. He was unlike a beech tree, under which nothing grows, but was a great and splendid oak, which fosters the flowers and undergrowth beneath it.

At this period, although the Liberals were nominally reunited, Lloyd George frequently found himself a lone voice, in sharp

Dole queue in 1924

disagreement with his own colleagues as well as with the Conservatives and the Socialists. For instance, in spite of his friendship
with Churchill, he strongly opposed his decision in 1925 as
Chancellor of the Exchequer, to restore the gold standard by re-
establishing the old parity between the dollar and sterling. This
involved raising the value of the pound by at least ten per cent,
thus making exports, especially coal, more difficult to sell overseas.
In this, he was supported by Sir Robert Horne, a former Chancellor of the Exchequer in the old Coalition, and some of the
younger Conservatives, notably Boothby. When the coal-owners
were led to reduce miners' wages, this was the direct result of
revaluation. Consequently he claimed that the General Strike of
1926, with all its dangers, was not only badly handled by Baldwin,
but the direct consequence of Churchill's policy. All this, which he
maintained with his usual vivacity, led to a bitter quarrel with
Asquith, Lord Grey and the other Liberal leaders. In addition, he
was bitterly critical of the Conservative Government's unwilling-
ness to face, and inability to remedy, the urgent problem of unemployment. For all through this Parliament the figures had stood
between one million and one and a half million. In view of the
limited relief afforded by the so-called 'dole', the consequent
sufferings in the most affected areas were terrible. Almost as
serious was the effect on the national expenditure. Since my own

constituency, Stockton-on-Tees, was, like all the north-east area, one of the most afflicted, I naturally sympathised with Lloyd George's strictures, although my friends and I were still content with unofficial protests and murmuring, and had not yet broken into open rebellion. But Lloyd George, with his extraordinary energy, did not content himself with occasional protests in the House of Commons. He published, with the help of expert advisers, four of the most remarkable state papers ever produced by a private individual. In their preparation he made free use of his own political fund – the best purpose to which it was ever put.

The first of these was the report of a Committee of M.P.s, industrialists, economists and engineers, appointed in March 1924. It appeared in the late summer. It rejected both syndicalism (the mines for the miners) and nationalisation. But it urged the purchase by the Government of all royalties – there were 4,000 separate owners – way-leaves and other rights affecting coal production. (This was, at least in part, carried out by the National Government after 1931.) It recommended the formation, out of the mass of separate undertakings, of groups of companies scientifically organised to exploit coal to the best advantage, to which the Government would grant leases. It also recommended the building of large power plants to increase the supply of electricity both for urban and rural areas, for the age of electricity must soon follow the age of steam.

Naturally both the great parties rejected the report with scorn. Part of it was applied, too late. Had it been adopted as a whole, the nation might have gained enormously – and the miners also.

The Land and the Nation with similar large proposals, followed the next year and was more revolutionary. 'The Green Book' (as it was popularly known) recommended in effect nationalisation of all agricultural land, chiefly on the ground that neither landlords nor tenants could find the necessary capital. But it did not face the issue of free imports or devise a system of prices such as has subsequently restored prosperity to agriculture. The result of this report was really to produce fresh quarrels within the Liberal Party.

Next came *Britain's Industrial Future* ('The Yellow Book') with imaginative, if sweeping, plans for modernisation and re-organisation – or rationalisation, as it came to be called – of British industry. Much of this was on lines similar to those which I had begun to follow, and which served me in the preparation of my books *Reconstruction* and *The Middle Way*, the latter published in 1938. During this period, Lloyd George used to ask me to his room in the House of Commons and expound his ideas with the enthusiasm and even excitement of a young man. He was now about sixty-five.

Finally, the culminating document in this series, *We Can Conquer Unemployment*, was launched in preparation for the General Election of 1929. This was the most remarkable, the most moderate, and the best argued of the series. Its contributors included such men as Maynard Keynes, Walter Layton, Hubert Henderson and Josiah Stamp – the leading economists in the country. Seebohm Rowntree and other industrialists took their full part.

In January 1929 unemployment had risen to about one and a half million. Baldwin and his Ministers deplored this, but found it difficult to find any solution which did not contradict their pre-judices or their pledges. Even Churchill could not withstand the pressure of the Treasury and the Bank of England, deeply wedded to a monetary policy which was either deflationary or at best opposed to any large increase in the quantity of money. The whole Government, and especially Churchill, were bound by the Election pledges of 1924 to a broadly Free Trade policy. Nevertheless, the Lloyd George proposals when revealed received wide support. It seemed intolerable, even on material grounds, that such large resources of men and equipment should rot away unused, when there was so much that needed doing to modernise the 'infra-structure', if ever we were to prosper again. On humanitarian grounds it was a double crime. The amount of national credit which would be required to launch a whole variety of schemes was well within our grasp, especially with such large sums lying idle in the banks, at a period when the rate of saving was outrunning the rate of investment. If the Socialists clung to theory and the

Conservatives refused to move, could not, Lloyd George argued, all reasonable men and women be induced to rally round a policy both pragmatic and imaginative? It was his last great attempt – but it failed utterly. Although the Liberal Party was more or less united, only 59 Liberals were returned, against 260 Conservatives, and 288 Socialists.

It was a staggering blow for Baldwin (the Conservatives fell from 400 to 260) and only a short triumph for MacDonald (the Labour Party rose from 162 to 288) – for his Government collapsed in ignominy two years later. For Lloyd George it was the end. In spite of a gallant effort six years later, it was clear that he could never return to power as the head of a party.

I shall never forget the Election of May 1929. I had to defend in Stockton the Conservative policy under the feeble slogan, 'Safety First'. But my unhappy constituents did not want 'Safety' – which meant hanging about the streets or haunting the factories in despair. Safety mean the 'dole'. They wanted work. So they very properly voted me out, and I had to confess, in my heart, that I could not blame them. There was no ill-feeling, for both my wife and I were popular. But there was a grim determination to demand a change. Alas, in a sense, they were destined to face still worse conditions, for many bitter years, before the tide began to turn.

In spite of all these disappointments, this man who had held office for seventeen consecutive years and reached the heights of fame, never showed any but the greatest good humour. He did not seem to resent his own impotence. Yet he was a giant among pygmies. To what was his failure due? First to the causes I have already described, the lack of machine, of a strong party and thus of a political base. In war a Minister can survive temporarily as a national leader; but in peace he must have the secure foundation of a party in the House of Commons and in the country. But there was perhaps a second reason. For all his great qualities one was conscious of a flaw. He was too quick, too versatile, too imaginative to command the trust of the English people. They liked something which seemed more solid, at any rate for times of peace. He enjoyed

The Election Pictorial

Incorporating
The LAND, MINING and INDUSTRIAL NEWS.

WE *CAN* CONQUER UNEMPLOYMENT

UNEMPLOYMENT MUST BE CONQUERED

These pictures, showing the tragedy of unemployment, emphasise the urgent need for a sound policy—the Liberal policy, as outlined by Mr. Lloyd George—to prevent the continuance of this human misery. The pictures show:

(1) An unemployed man sleeping on the Thames Embankment.

(2) One of thousands of queues of despondent men waiting at an Employment Exchange for a job—or the dole.

(3) Children in an industrial area clamouring for food.

(4) A "soup queue" of unemployed outside a charity institution.

The Liberal Party is pledged to remedy these evils, if you give it the chance (see pages 2, 3 and 8).

the admiration of all; but in a curious way he was unable to obtain that trust which is necessary for a national leader except, perhaps, at a time of proved disaster. Baldwin, who was as sensitive an artist and as highly-strung a character as Lloyd George himself, was able to conceal all this under the outward appearance of passivity, with his pipe, his country life and all the rest. He could assume without difficulty an appearance of that dull respectability that carries weight. Lloyd George was not respectable in the old middle-class sense. He was a genius with all the faults of genius, in private and even in public life. Yet as Churchill truly said in his tribute after Lloyd George's death, 'When the English history of the first quarter of the twentieth century is written, it will be seen that the greater part of our fortunes in peace and war were shaped by this one man.'

III

After the Election of 1929 I did not see Lloyd George, except on one or two chance occasions of a social character. I had lost my seat, and was trying to find some rapid way back to the House by a by-election. When this attempt proved abortive, I determined to try to win back Stockton. Naturally, I did not know how soon the opportunity would come or how easy the contest would be.

For during the two years, from 1929 to 1931, partly owing to the general recession in the world, partly by the collapse of the American boom, and partly by their own incompetence, Mac-Donald's Government grew steadily weaker. Lloyd George tried to use the Liberal group, which in theory at least could do so, to play a decisive part. But the instrument broke in his hands, and even began to disintegrate. Meanwhile, conditions in the country grew steadily worse. In December 1930 the unemployment figure rose to two and a half million, and even in the following summer – when there is generally some improvement – remained at that terrible total. A financial crisis was looming ahead. Nothing relieved the gloom in Parliament except the rhetorical duels between

Unemployed miners searching for coal on a coal tip

Churchill and Snowden (the Labour Chancellor of the Exchequer). They were well matched.

By a fatal chance Lloyd George was taken ill and had to submit to a severe operation at the very moment when Ramsay MacDonald, the Labour Prime Minister, was meditating the break-up of his Government (for most of whom he had little liking) in order to form a National Government to face the impending crisis. For several weeks rumour was rife, and it was clear that in any all-party administration Lloyd George must play a leading part. But it was not to be. There was only one moment in the twenty years of his eclipse when Lloyd George could have returned to power. When the chance returned, in 1940, he was too old and too weak.

Since Churchill was also excluded from the National Government, from this moment until the outbreak of the Second World War, the two most notable men in the House of Commons, with the longest experience and the greatest capacity to handle great events, were on the back benches. The mediocrities reigned supreme, and immovable.

The formation of the National Government in August 1931, and still more the General Election in October marked the end of all Lloyd George's hopes. The Conservatives, 473 of whom were elected, swept the board. The Liberals were reduced to 37, Labour to 52. He denounced the holding of the election contrary to the assurances which he had received from MacDonald in August, as 'a partisan intrigue under guise of a patriotic appeal.'

By the end of 1934, he began to work on a new project. In view of the overwhelming majority supporting the MacDonald–Baldwin regime, many efforts were made, in and out of the House, to organise some kind of forward movement, to get us out of the trough, which might gain support from 'men and women of all parties and of none'. By the beginning of 1932, the unemployment figure had almost reached three million. In the next three years the figures were 2,400,000, 2,300,000 and 2,300,000, with some fall in the summer months. Although the measures taken had certainly stabilised sterling (after devaluation) and restored some degree of financial confidence, and the fiscal measures were giving support to the home trade, yet the great exporting businesses were almost in collapse, with corresponding effects on the areas in which they were situated.

I have described in *Winds of Change* the contribution which my friends and I tried to make to these movements for a more imaginative policy. They culminated in the work of The Next Five Years Group, whose report, with a large number of distinguished signatories, was published in July 1935. Lloyd George's New Deal was launched in January 1935, mainly anticipating our publication. Since he claimed that his appeal was 'non-party' – and an appeal to public opinion rather than a last bid for power, no difficulties arose. Indeed some of us had many meetings with him either in his London office or at Churt.

The Chairman of The Next Five Years Group was Lord Allen of Hurtwood, under whose enthusiastic leadership a remarkable body of men was brought together. He was a man with a strange background and a most unusual career. An extreme Socialist, he was a conscientious objector during the war, and later became Chairman of the Independent Labour Party. In 1931 he supported MacDonald, and later received a peerage. Cursed by ill-health, he never spared himself. I can still see his noble head, spare – almost cadaverous. He began as a fanatic; but he had received now a new light. He became fanatical for moderation.

In fact, Lloyd George's proposals (or those of his committee) were neither so well worked-out nor so novel as our own, but they were on similar lines. Indeed in the early months of the year, while the Government still professed itself ready to examine the Lloyd George plans seriously, a number of Conservatives – Lord Londonderry, Lord Eustace Percy, Sir Arthur Steel-Maitland as well as Churchill – gave their support. I, as member for Stockton still suffering so grievously, did so with enthusiasm. Later on, in order to promulgate the New Deal, Lloyd George founded the 'Council of Action' drawn from a wide range of sympathisers. The Government had proved very lukewarm, even hostile. He was therefore quite entitled to start this organisation, which he supported

with considerable sums from his fund and all the regular apparatus
of a political movement.

During this period, at my meetings with Lloyd George, whether
alone or with others, I was struck by a great change. He was now
an old man (he was 72) and showed signs of weariness and irritation,
being less ready to listen and more easily upset by contradiction.
Nevertheless, he retained, in general, his buoyancy and charm.
His operation (as I was to know later to my cost) left its mark.
The marvel was that he remained so keen and active.

Meanwhile, in the course of the summer, some difficulties had
arisen in The Next Five Years Group, some of whom, no doubt,
were not admirers of Lloyd George. This situation led to some
difficulty. Certain confidential discussions were held just before
publication of our book as to whether Lloyd George should become a signatory. We did not want, as Clifford Allen remarked,
the New Deal to turn out a New Game. It was therefore decided
not to ask him to sign but to let things develop. Lloyd George's
next step was to form 'Councils of Action for Peace and Reconstruction' and to initiate a campaign of meetings throughout the
country. For myself, I was quite prepared to appear on a non-party
platform, on the understanding that it really was non-party, and
I was followed in this by other Conservative Members. Consequently I attended the first meeting at the Central Hall. But
with the approaching Election the situation clearly became both
delicate and embarrassing. Allen, Crowther, Sir Walter Layton,
and I, representing the group, saw Lloyd George on 12 August
at Churt. Naturally this tea-party fluttered the political dovecotes
and caused a great excitement in the Press. There had been much
talk about the formation of a new Centre Party; but of course
this was quite impracticable, and was never at any time con-
templated. As a result of our discussion, we recommended to our
colleagues that we ought not to participate as a group (whatever
individuals might do), because such an action would be contrary
to the spirit of our original constitution. For myself, being perhaps
less squeamish, I found no difficulty in welcoming the Council of
Action and I attended the inaugural meeting on 1 July 1935.

It took place in the Church Hall, Westminster, in very respectable surroundings and under equally respectable patronage. At any rate, I found myself once more in the honoured company of Lord Robert Cecil.

But the Election was approaching, and the ponderous forces of the National Government, now almost entirely Conservative, were able to present a good enough case to hold their support in the prosperous parts of the country and to lose only marginally even in the distressed areas. Nor was it altogether a bad or unconvincing story. If much remained to be done, much had been achieved. Moreover, the great issue of Mussolini's attack on Abyssinia and the Government's loyal – almost fanatical – devotion to the League of Nations, together with its readiness to support the League in any steps, however drastic, to oppose the aggressive dictator – all this paralysed the Labour Party (who were led by pacifists) and outflanked the Liberals.

Therefore, although the Council of Action issued a 'questionnaire' to all candidates and exerted some pressure in this way, it had little effect on the result. For my part, I had determined to fight in Stockton on the basis of The Next Five Years plan, and on this policy I was able to hold the seat, which I had won back in 1931, by a majority of 4,000 over a strong Labour candidate, Miss Susan Lawrence. A Liberal stood, but forfeited his deposit.

Lloyd George was almost shattered by the result of the General Election, where in spite of a rise in Labour Members from 52 to 154, the Conservatives still held an unshakable majority, with 432 supporters. The Liberals (that is the official Liberals) were reduced to 23. From this time on he ceased to play the role of a party leader. He had stood at Caernarvon as an Independent Liberal. His personal triumph was complete – but he had no organised following, and he knew it. What neither he nor any of us knew was that there would not be another General Election for ten years, and then after the most terrible war in history.

Between 1935 and 1940 – when at last the Conservative majority rebelled against its leader – I would see Lloyd George from time to time. Sometimes he would ask me to his room, or his office, or to Churt. But, except for rare moments when the old genius burst out – usually in rage – he seemed now rather quiet, as one who has lost his way. His judgment too became erratic, and his friends often could not dissuade him from a foolish course. Such was his famous visit to Germany and his meeting with Hitler. Since this took place after the fatal re-militarisation of the Rhineland in 1936 (which in effect made it impossible for France to redeem her promises to Eastern Europe and was a complete breach of Germany's plighted word), the visit, which was naturally publicised all over the world, had a deplorable effect, both at home and abroad. Nevertheless, in spite of these dark blunders, there were some sparkling moments still. I remember his speech in June 1936, when the Government which had been elected to stop Mussolini in Abyssinia surrendered at Geneva. Sanctions, never honestly or effectively imposed, were abandoned – apparently at the bidding of the Chancellor of the Exchequer, Neville Chamberlain. Our Foreign Secretary, Samuel Hoare, had already been dismissed as the forfeit for the Government's betrayal of its pledges; the next, Eden, had no doubt to yield to the harsh pressure of realities. Nevertheless, I felt so incensed that a few days later I wrote to Baldwin resigning the Whip. In this historic debate, Baldwin cut a very poor figure. I think the Hoare–Laval episode a few months earlier had shaken him. Hoare had been brought back into the Government a few weeks before, after an adulatory speech about Baldwin; this was not popular in the Conservative Party, who thought the boots of Prime Ministers should be licked in private. Lloyd George said that

> It is true that he [Hoare] had a reassurance that he would be brought back after a period of quarantine, and when he comes back he finds the wind tempered to the bleating lamb.

He went on to say these terrible words in his most formidable tones:

> I have been in this House very nearly half-a-century ... I have never before heard a British Minister, one holding the most important position in the Government next to the Prime Minister at the present

Greeting Hitler   *Speaking in 1939*

moment, come down to the House of Commons and say that Britain was beaten, Britain and her Empire beaten, and that we must abandon an enterprise we had taken in hand.

His most powerful blows were reserved for Baldwin. He quoted the Prime Minister's speech to the Peace Society: 'Let your aim be resolute and your footsteps firm and certain,' and made devastating play with these words.

Here is the resolute aim; here is the certain footstep – running away . . . this speech, which was delivered on the eve of the Election, was delivered to assure the world that we stand by our pledges. Only a few weeks after the Election was over, they were negotiating treachery to their pledges. Fifty nations ranged themselves behind that torch. They said, 'Here is the British Prime Minister, with the greatest Empire in the world marching; we will range ourselves behind him.' The Abyssinians believed it; the vast majority of the people of this country believed it. The Government had not been in for more than a few weeks before that torch was dimmed. Tonight it is quenched – with a hiss; a hiss that will be re-echoed throughout the whole world.

Nobody who heard it can ever forget the extraordinary power and scorn, enhanced by the Welsh intonation into which he always fell in moments of excitement, of the word 'hiss'. He ended by turning on Neville Chamberlain and quoted his election speech, and his words reflected on Chamberlain's recent assumption of the right to announce the Government's foreign policy.

The speech of the Chancellor of the Exchequer has been quoted. I am going to do myself the honour of reading a part of it again. The right hon. Gentleman is heir to the throne and recently he has been trying the crown on to see how it fits. I hope for his own sake that it does not. He has not merely tried the crown on. He has wielded the sceptre – which is just the sort of thing that heirs do when there are weak monarchs. The right hon. Gentleman said at the last election:
'The choice before us is whether we shall make a last effort at Geneva for peace and security or whether by a cowardly surrender we shall break all the promises we have made and hold ourselves up to the shame of our children and their children's children.'
Tonight we have had the cowardly surrender, and *there* are the cowards.

Churchill is on record as having described this speech as one of the greatest Parliamentary performances of all time. But this was almost his last great effort, as the old man knew. This is, perhaps, why he put so much of his power and genius into it.

As during these grim years we drifted through threatening clouds and storms in Europe, there was at least some relief gained for the manufacturing industries from the modest degree of re-armament to which the Baldwin, and later the Chamberlain Government could be pushed. Lloyd George seemed now unable to reach the clear decisions to which his friends had been accustomed. Similarly, when the Molotov–Ribbentrop Pact came in August 1939, he was more and more uncertain. He had not planned the course of events; his advice, like Churchill's, had been set aside or laughed at. What should he now do? And during the so-called 'phoney war', although Churchill had accepted the call from those who had so long ignored him, Lloyd George had received no summons. One last service he was to give to the nation. In the critical debate of 7–8 May 1940 – a few days before Hitler's onslaught on Western Europe – the Prime Minister, Chamberlain, was bitterly attacked by Leo Amery, an old friend and a Birmingham Member. In reply, he was rash enough to call on his friends – 'and I still have some friends' – to rally to him. It is said that Lloyd George had not meant to speak until this incident was repeated to him while he was resting in his room. He did not wish to injure Churchill who, as First Lord of the Admiralty, carried a heavy responsibility for the failure in Norway. So he got round his difficulty by appealing to him not to let himself be made 'an air-raid shelter to keep the splinters from hitting his colleagues'.

Lloyd George knew that, whatever might be Chamberlain's merits (and Lloyd George thought little of them) such a man could never be a War Minister. He was worse than Asquith – more obstinate and not so clever. So, as usual, he struck at the main target.

It is not a question of who are the Prime Minister's friends. It is a far larger issue . . . He has asked for sacrifice. The nation is prepared for every sacrifice so long as it has leadership. I say solemnly that the Prime Minister should give an example of sacrifice, because there is nothing which can contribute more to victory than that he should sacrifice the seals of office.

During 1940 and 1941 Churchill made genuine efforts to secure Lloyd George's co-operation. But he hesitated – for what reason it is hard to be sure. When I saw him after the fall of France, he seemed very pessimistic, almost defeatist. He was now an old man, over seventy-five, and he shrank, I think, from the logic of events. Hitler had deceived him – or perhaps had Lloyd George wished to be deceived? After all, much of Hitler's internal reconstruction followed the principles of Lloyd George's New Deal, and he was both admiring and envious.

In the years before and following Munich he was pessimistic.

Having rightly formed the view that the only hope of stopping Germany was by an alliance with Russia, he was impatient at the apparent delays and hesitations of British policy, without, perhaps, understanding all the difficulties. When, in March 1939, the British Government, in disgust with Hitler's gross breach of faith, began to distribute guarantees – first to Poland, then to Rumania, and finally to Greece, Lloyd George gave his solemn warning, 'Without Russia, these three guarantees . . . are the most reckless commitment that any country has ever entered into. I will say more. They are demented pledges, that cannot be redeemed . . .' Of course, as so often, he offended his audience, but he was right. Once again, his fears were justified. How could we win without Russia? How could he, or any of us, believe that Hitler would suddenly attack Russia.

But perhaps in reality, his real feeling was that he had little at seventy-seven or seventy-eight to give. He had held the supreme position in war. What could he do now? He was old; he was tired; he was irritable. He knew in his heart that he had nothing more to contribute – nothing, at any rate, worthy of his powers. For nearly twenty years he had been out of office. He had made great efforts. He had put forward almost the only new and constructive idea which had emerged during the long years of depression and decay. They had all been rejected with scorn. Let them get on without him.

Yet many of his friends, including his oldest friend, Churchill, urged him, with persistence, to join them. The Prime Minister offered him a place in the War Cabinet, where he could contribute from his experience without the burden of a department. But the offer was, perhaps a little unfortunately, made 'subject to the approval of Neville Chamberlain'. This condition aroused the old man's fury. He replied, in an indignant letter, setting out his grievances. In their talk, according to Lloyd George, Churchill had made it quite clear that if Chamberlain interposed his veto, on the ground of personal resentment over past differences, he could not proceed with the offer.

'This is not a firm offer. Until it is definite, I cannot consider it.'

Churchill sent a soothing reply, and referred to the possible use of Lloyd George's services in connection with food production. It must be remembered that Churchill's position was delicate. He had long been out of favour with the greater part of the Conservatives. Chamberlain was Leader of the Party, holding a position in the War Coalition analogous to that of Bonar Law. It was only after Chamberlain's death in the autumn, that Churchill was elected to the leadership.

Beaverbrook continued to press Lloyd George to join the War Cabinet, which he felt sure could be arranged. So did his other friends, including Leo Amery, Boothby and myself. But it was no good. He seemed to have lost his will-power, and to live always in the past.

In December 1940, after Lord Lothian's death in Washington, where he had been a most successful Ambassador, Churchill tried again. Why should not Lloyd George take this important post – never more important than at this moment, the crisis of our history?

He was attracted; hesitated; consulted his doctors; then refused.

In January 1941 his wife, Dame Margaret, died at Criccieth. He was prevented, owing to terrible blizzards and snowdrifts, from reaching her death-bed in time. He arrived, at last, in a state of collapse. It was a cruel blow.

Throughout 1941 he became more and more depressed, even defeatist. In May there was a painful incident in the House of Commons. Lloyd George made a long, rather rambling speech, certainly without any suggestion of peace. Churchill, himself under great strain amid all the perils of the day, criticised it sharply, even saying that it might have been delivered by Pétain in the last days of Reynaud's Cabinet. It may well be that much of Lloyd George's attitude in private conversation had reached Churchill's ears, and he decided to put a stop to such dangerous talk.

I did not see him again after I went to Algiers in 1942. I did not want to trouble him with letters although I perhaps might have given him a passing pleasure. For he liked to be remembered.

Finally, in October 1943, he married Miss Frances Stevenson. As the war seemed to be drawing to its close, and an election would certainly follow, he had to decide whether he would fight Caernarvon, which he had held for more than fifty years. Since he clearly could not stand a campaign physically, he accepted an earldom in January 1945. In fact, he need not have worried about any more elections, for he died peacefully at the age of eighty-two on 26 March 1945.

Amidst the stirring events of those tremendous days even Lloyd George's death caused but a ripple. To use Talleyrand's cruel epigram about Napoleon's death at St Helena, 'It was no longer an event; only a piece of news.'

Yet even for those who only knew Lloyd George after his days of power, in the brilliant autumn and sad winter of his life, it *was* an event, like the crashing of a great oak in the forest.

CHAPTER THREE

Ramsay MacDonald

HISTORIANS will regard the rise of the Labour Party in the first quarter of the twentieth century as the most dramatic change in the long history of party politics in England. Roundheads and Cavaliers, Whigs and Tories, Liberals and Conservatives – there had always been a division into two contending forces. Each, of course, had their own internal differences and groups, ranging from the moderate to the extreme, or sometimes based on family or local interests. Yet the natural tendency to split into two main divisions had operated from the time of Charles I. Moreover, the fact that the House of Commons met originally in a chapel and afterwards in a chamber based upon the same ground plan made it natural for men to think in these simple terms. Those on the right of Mr Speaker were for the Government of the day; those on the left were against; and however many might be the varying sections within each grouping yet two main parties with changing names, and indeed often changing policies, divided the country. In a word the chamber was rectangular like a church, not circular like a theatre. The differences between the political development in Britain and that in most European countries depends on this simple fact.

It is true that the House of Commons was enlivened for many years by the exuberance of the large and turbulent Irish Party, which cut across the normal political structure and was adept, especially if the two main parties were nicely balanced, in intrigue with both sides in turn. It is also true that among the members who owed allegiance or followed the guidance of the long Whig rule from the first to the second Reform Bill, the radicals formed a separate body and could sometimes be cajoled by the wiles of so shrewd a parliamentarian as Disraeli into abandoning the Whig leaders, at least temporarily. Nevertheless, Britain was normally governed, and on the whole liked to be governed, by a two-party system. People understood it. Their sporting instincts made them feel that politics was only another form of contest more exciting than cricket, although less spectacular than football. Everything led to the acceptance of two parties alternately in power.

In the Election of 1900 there emerged a small group of members known as Labour members, put forward largely by the help of certain trade unions. There were only two at the beginning of the Parliament; by the time of the dissolution there were four. In 1906 the number rose to thirty. There were also a few called Lib-Lab, radicals relying on trade union sympathy. But this phenomenon was only like a small cloud no bigger than a man's hand, and when it first emerged in the years before the First World War few except, curiously enough, Balfour recognised its significance. There was, of course, a radical group in the Liberal Party, and these no doubt tended to collaborate with their Labour or Lib-Lab colleagues. Indeed they were able to exert their power quite dramatically in forcing a Liberal Government, in spite of its immense majority, to yield to their demands over the Trade Disputes Bill of 1906, which restored to the trade unions powers which the courts had challenged, and added many privileges, such as the right of 'picketing'. All this held the seeds of future dangers. Nevertheless until 1914 the two-party system seemed unshaken and unshakable. The Lib-Lab and Labour group members would be no different in their relationship with the Liberal Party than had been the old radicals, like Cobden and Bright towards Whigs such as Lord John Russell. They would grumble, bring pressure to bear, bargain, occasionally blackmail; but in the main they would see to it that a Liberal Government remained in power or that a Liberal Opposition was not broken up. Yet by 1923 a Labour Government was formed, which although

Ramsay MacDonald in 1907

in a minority in the House of Commons was still a true Labour
Government, independent both of Conservatives and Liberals.
How had this come about? Undoubtedly the main contributors
to this unprecedented change were the Founding Fathers – Keir
Hardie, George Barnes, Arthur Henderson and Ramsay Mac-
Donald. These, together with Philip Snowden and others, took
the lead. It was by their almost Machiavellian skill that these men
who had embraced the principles of what they called Socialism,
managed to foist their doctrine on the main trade unions and thus
create a political and parliamentary party almost at a single blow.
Replacing the painful task of slowly building up a party in the
traditional sense by local organisations and the like, they succeeded,
by persuasion, in possessing themselves of the control of a number
of powerful trade unions, contrary to the tradition and, as many
believed, the proper functions of trade unionism. In this way and
by disregarding the wishes of many trade unionists who were
staunch Liberals or Conservatives the Labour Party sprang almost
ready armed into the field. As the years passed the new party was
able to increase its hold upon the trade unions. It became their
masters, with, of course, the danger of ultimately becoming their
servants. This spectacular change which led to the first Labour
Government did not seem as yet to carry with it the dangers which
have recently become more apparent. Now this Frankenstein's
monster seems to threaten not merely the parties of the Right and
Centre but its own child, the party of the Left. Thus by a series
of skilful manoeuvres MacDonald and his associates were able to
turn the Labour movement into a political organisation in Parliament. But there was much to assist them. The trade unions up to
then had been unwilling to get involved with party politics.
Indeed they frankly admitted that they had gained many of their
ambitions – shorter hours and other social reforms – from Liberal
and especially from Conservative Governments, partly by persuasion, partly by pressure. In 1906 and subsequent years many
did not wish to be the catspaw of a Liberal leader. But MacDonald
and Snowden looked far beyond the present. Gradually the trade
union movement could be persuaded, whatever its members might

individually feel, to develop into a party of their own supported by the funds collected from their members.

Yet it is doubtful whether this movement could have taken them to the position they achieved in 1923 to 1924 had it not been for the confusion and schism in the Liberal Party. It is true that the Asquithians and Lloyd Georgians came together, though unwillingly, on the basis of defending Free Trade in the General Election of 1923, when it was challenged by Baldwin and the Tories. But their unity was frail and their internecine quarrels were deep and soon resumed. Moreover, after the Election of 1924 it did not seem likely that a Liberal revival could take the form of a Liberal Government. They would never again have an overall majority. Indeed they were in a hopeless quandary. They could make no alliance with the Right (that is the Conservatives), without reverting to the Coalition, now regarded in the Liberal camp as a dirty word. To go to the Right would have been to justify Lloyd George and abandon Asquith. Similarly they could make no effective moves to the Left. Liberalism after all had always been the traditional defender of capitalism. The great industrialists of the nineteenth century – the iron-masters, the cotton-masters, the ship-owners and all the rest – were traditional Liberals; so was a large part of the banking and City interest. The Tories were identified with the land, the services and the Church, and the more sporting elements of the working classes. Even the brewers were quite late adherents. They had originally been the leading contributors to the Liberal Party funds. Therefore an alliance to the Left would mean a split in the Liberal Party. Nor would Asquith have approved of it. By a curious chance Lloyd George, who would have been the natural man to bring about a union between Left-Wing Liberalism and the rising Labour movement, was identified through the war years with the capitalist section of his party. Asquith, who might have been willing to co-operate with the Conservatives, by temperament and the moderation of his views, found it difficult to work with the Labour leaders, whom he intellectually despised and by whom he was continually rebuffed.

Thus it became clear in the year before I entered Parliament that the new organisation of British politics was difficult to operate and unsuited to the temperament of the British people. The three-party system was not likely to continue. The Liberal Party would decline, some going to Labour, others to the Conservatives. The high reputation of its great figures like Asquith and Lloyd George delayed this process, but could not prevent it. Thus the way stood open for the new Labour leaders; they were not slow to seize their opportunity.

Not having been elected to the 1923–1924 Parliament I saw MacDonald in operation only from the Gallery. After its rapid and rather inglorious fall in October 1924 I watched him for many years when he was leader of the Labour opposition. After the formation of the National Government in 1931 until his retirement in 1937 he became a familiar figure, whom I saw not only in the House but met on frequent social occasions. Much has been written about this strange man and his strange career. No full or formal biography has yet appeared, where his papers might be revealed. He has been violently attacked or strongly praised according to the point of view of the critic. Some regard him as a double-dyed traitor who destroyed his own child in 1931; others as a man of high patriotic motives who consciously took a decision which he knew would blacken his reputation but believed to be in the national interest. Where does the truth lie? The answer perhaps lies in the fact that by temperament he was a romantic. He was also vain and, like Sir Willoughby Patterne, he had a good leg. Born of humble origin in the East Highlands, he had all the pride and ambition of his race. He was not an economist, though he wrote a rather sentimental book on Socialism which I remember reading with some enthusiasm when I was at school. I am sure he had not studied Marxism.

When I first saw him he was a handsome man, with a most beautiful voice and an impressive manner. I never saw him on the platform, where I think he ranted. He certainly failed altogether on the radio. But in the House of Commons he was able to present, until the last years when his mind began to fail, a coherent argument

MacDonald the romantic   *At the microphone*

– and to present it with calm and dignity. He had shown his courage
in the years of the First War when he was Chairman of the Parliamentary Party. When the whole nation with almost universal
loyalty was sacrificing everything to beat the Germans, MacDonald
retained, in spite of its unpopularity, a pacifist position which
commanded only a few followers even in the extreme Socialist
movement. Snowden and some others followed him; but the
mass of the working classes and even the greater part of the trade
union machine supported the war.

When Lloyd George formed his great War Government in
1916 there was deep division among the Labour M.P.s. Ramsay

MacDonald, supported by Philip Snowden and Sidney Webb (who was a kind of father confessor to the party) were strongly opposed to joining. Lloyd George exercised all his charm, and a long discussion followed. By a vote of 17 to 14, after a stormy debate, MacDonald found himself in the minority. Arthur Henderson, who by a strange chance, was to be his chief opponent at the time of the formation of MacDonald's National Government in 1931, entered Lloyd George's War Administration. MacDonald was, however, elected, against Henderson, to the leadership in 1922. Henderson followed him in the leadership of the shattered party in 1931. How truly Churchill used to tell me that 'Politics are a steeple-chase, not a flat-race. You never know what will happen.' MacDonald therefore remained through the war, almost alone, abandoned by the greater part of his Socialist friends and subjected to many pressures, even insults, as a result of such a position in time of war. To be candid he had a natural tendency towards martyrdom. I do not believe he disliked this experience, any more than he did the reverse in 1931. He always seemed to me to enjoy and even exploit the troubles and worries of a Prime Minister. He would go about complaining that he felt like 'a weary titan'. Nevertheless that was only part of the histrionic side of his temperament. He was a good actor and like all good actors he threw himself completely into his part.

In the first Labour Government he showed unexpected qualities of statesmanship and began to get support from many moderate people who were anxious that this first experiment of a Labour Government should succeed. He made perhaps a mistake in combining the premiership with the Foreign Office. This was a heavy burden which even the great Lord Salisbury found difficult to sustain. But at any rate the latter operated from the House of Lords in a period when Parliament seldom lasted more than five or six months of the year, and without the difficulties of a balanced political situation with no clear majority in the House of Commons. MacDonald made a gallant effort to fulfil this double role. But I feel sure that the tactical mistakes which brought about his fall could easily have been handled without disaster. But he could not bear to take advice, most of all from the Liberals, on whose support his majority depended. The new minority Government had the usual difficulties and relied on Liberal help to sustain themselves against a numerically larger Conservative Party. But somehow, not even Asquith could get on with MacDonald. Lloyd George despised him, and soon began to complain of his vanity. Any criticism, he declared, however well-meant, was resented. Yet the Liberals were expected to be 'the oxen to drag Labour over the rough roads of Parliament for two or three years, and, at the end of the journey, when there is no further use for them, they are to be slaughtered.'

MacDonald's aims in foreign affairs commanded general support. The reconciliation of France and Germany set in motion a policy which became fruitful later on at Locarno, in the hands of Austen Chamberlain. His recognition of the Soviet Government followed precedent. When a Government was acknowledged to be in full possession and authority over its territory, it was in accordance with tradition to grant it recognition.

But he became embarrassed in a long and difficult negotiation about the question of Russia's debts to Britain and her anxiety to obtain a large British loan. A loan might help unemployment here; but at what cost seemed uncertain.

He now began to appear to men of moderate views as too sub-servient to his own extremists. The story of the Russian Treaty, where negotiations were first broken off and then re-started under Left-Wing pressure, was followed by MacDonald first refusing a loan to Russia, and then granting it, apparently from the same motive. There followed the incident of the Campbell case, which seeming at first trivial, brought about the defeat of the first Labour Government. Here a prosecution had been instituted by the Attorney-General against a Communist agitator, for circulating subversive pamphlets to the troops. The prosecution was with-drawn, apparently again under extreme Socialist pressure. The Prime Minister's answers were equivocal, and the Conservatives tabled a vote of censure. The Liberals, hoping to find a way out for the Government, proposed a select Committee of Enquiry.

MacDonald angrily rejected this, and Baldwin astutely withdrew his vote of censure (for which the Liberals would not have voted) and put his people into the lobby in support of the Liberal proposal (for which they could scarcely avoid voting). Thus the Government were defeated, and immediately asked for a Dissolution.

The 1924 Election was complicated and obscured by an issue which came to be known as the matter of the Zinoviev letter. The text of what appeared to be a confidential communication from Zinoviev, as President of the Third International, to the British Communist Party had fallen into the hands of the Foreign Office. It was the usual inflammatory and subversive stuff. Perhaps the most dangerous passages were those referring to the creation of revolutionary cells in the fighting services. In view of the recent and friendly negotiations between the British and Russian Governments, a note of protest seemed called for. The Foreign Office advised MacDonald in favour of publication of the text of the letter, all the more because the *Daily Mail* was known to have obtained a copy and would undoubtedly publish it before the end of the election. But here again poor MacDonald's luck was out. The letter has recently been shown to be a fake, but MacDonald was advised by the Foreign Office that it was genuine and made some fumbling excuses about it in the last days of the election. Added to other examples of maladroitness and muddle, the Red Letter came as the final piece of testimony of the unfitness to govern of MacDonald and his friends.

At the General Election, MacDonald's party was defeated, but largely because so many Liberal seats were lost to the Conservatives. Labour fell from 193 to 151; Liberals from 158 to 40. Conservatives rose from 259 to 419. Among the fortunate beneficiaries of MacDonald's failures was the honourable Member for Stockton on Tees, who thus entered Parliament for the first time.

Through the following years, 1924 to 1929, I was to watch MacDonald with interest from my place on the Tory back-benches. His speeches, chiefly on foreign affairs, were a little rambling, but always impressive. His fine head, his noble presence and his beautifully modulated voice gave him an air of authority. But already it was becoming very difficult to know what he really was. Was he a Socialist? He certainly was not a Marxist. In some ways I felt that he was much nearer to the old Christian Socialist ideals of my grandfather. That is to say his political attitude was not based on clear economic concepts, but much more upon the general demands of humanity, with especial regard to the needs of the poor and those who had fallen by the wayside. The more you listened to MacDonald the more fascinated you became by the cadence of his voice and the musical phrases of his oratory. But it was difficult to discern any very specific purpose, or any clear conclusions. On special issues where he was attacking Government policy and his mind could be made to focus on to a narrower front he could be effective; but even here he would seem always ready to be tempted away from the particular to the general.

In April 1925 I had a short passage at arms with him in the House. During the recess MacDonald had made an appeal to the 'Young Conservatives' to cross the floor and join the really progressive party. Of course it was very flattering to be noticed at all, after so short a Parliamentary experience. I thought it too good an opportunity to miss, and in the course of my maiden speech on 30 April 1925 I ventured to take up the challenge.

I should like, if it be not impertinent, to say this. The Leader of the Opposition, in remarks made during the Recess, made an appeal to some of the younger and more progressive Members of the Conservative party to range themselves under his flag. I well understand that the general of an army, half of which is reputed to be in mutiny, and the other half in a state more or less of passive despair, should wish to find some new recruits, but I can assure him . . . that, if he thinks that we are either so young or so inexperienced as to be caught by a trap so clumsy as his, it shows that he totally misunderstands the moral principles and ideals of democratic Toryism. He has no conception of what those ideals and principles mean to us. If he thinks that he and his party have only to offer us as the true socialism a kind of mixture, a sort of horrible political cocktail, consisting partly of the dregs of exploded economic views of Karl Marx, mixed up with a little flavour of Cobdenism, well iced by the late Chancellor of the Exchequer, and with a little ginger from the Member for the Gorbals [Mr. Buchanan] – if he thinks that this is to be the draught given to our parched throats and that we are ready to accept it, he is very much mistaken.

Nevertheless, the first Labour Government was a remarkable achievement. MacDonald had brought a party to power in a single generation, and himself to the highest office. Yet, partly from his dislike for the Liberals, his tenure was brief. He had a natural sympathy for the Conservative Party, especially the Tory and aristocratic elements. It was said by some that this ultimately destroyed him. But he was not a mere snob or tuft-hunter. He had in himself an aristocratic element based upon vision, imagination and dreams. His antipathy to the Liberal Party was partly jealousy of the traditional party of the Left, and partly because he looked back to the Liberalism which represented the bosses, the hard-headed industrialists, the Mr Gradgrinds, who had repulsed all the claims of Labour and rejected all reforms, whether on intellectual grounds (like John Morley's extreme devotion to *laissez-faire*) or on grounds of personal advantage. Towards the Tories, especially the land-owning Tories he had no such feelings.

After the Conservative defeat in 1929, when I lost my seat, I saw little of MacDonald except occasionally at the house of my dear friends, Lord and Lady Londonderry. Because Wynyard was so close to Stockton on Tees, my wife and I had found there a ready respite from the exhaustion of our labours in the constituency. Since Seaham Harbour was MacDonald's seat (and Seaham was Londonderry property), he was equally entertained and cared for, in spite of his Socialist opinions, for the Londonderrys were large-hearted people, intelligent and broadminded. Lady Londonderry soon became a real friend to me, and an equally loyal supporter in good or bad times. To MacDonald she showed a sympathy which some thought constituted a temptation which lured him to his fall.

In any event, I did not follow closely the story of the second Labour Government, from May 1929 to August 1931. I was busy in my own affairs, and my colleagues who had kept their seats were busy in trying either to dislodge or prop up their leader, Baldwin.

Perhaps all parties are bad losers. But certainly the Conservatives are apt to seek scapegoats for defeat either in the Leader or the party organisation. In 1930 and 1931 Baldwin had a rough time; but by August 1931 he had ridden the storm and was able to sail his holiday bark quietly to the smooth backwater of Aix-les-Bains. Then, in August 1931 came the crisis – financial and political, followed by the collapse of the Labour Administration and the formation of an all-party Government. Its announced purpose was to deal with the pressing and critical issues and then bring itself to an end. In fact it lasted, under different forms but the same name – National – until May 1940, when it perished ingloriously, to be replaced by Churchill's great War Coalition.

It was MacDonald's misfortune that the Chancellor of the Exchequer, Philip Snowden, so far from following Socialist or even expansionist policies, was wedded to the most rigid orthodoxy, almost worthy of Mr Gladstone himself. Thus he insisted on maintaining, or at least appearing to maintain a 'sound' Budget, even including a contribution of some £50 million to the Sinking Fund. Modern readers will probably have forgotten even the meaning of this term. In those unregenerate days it was thought to be a sound principle of public, as well as of private finance, to avoid increasing debt and gradually to pay off existing debt from taxation. This was before the concept of deficit financing or hire purchase. In addition Snowden insisted on some drastic economies in public expenditure. All the Cabinet accepted the principle; the difficulty came about its application. Judges and civil servants, officers and men in the services were to be docked ten per cent. But what about the enormous debt of the Unemployment Fund, which provided payments for the unemployed? After much wrangling about the detail (about which there was some obscurity and much subsequent argument regarding what individual Ministers had or had not been willing to accept) MacDonald decided to go to the Palace and offer the resignation of the Labour Administration. He was given authority to form a new one on all-party lines.

The literature surrounding these and subsequent events is large and comprehensive. The two outstanding facts which chiefly interested me were: first, that Lloyd George, from illness, and Churchill, owing to his previous resignation from Baldwin's 'Shadow Cabinet' on the India question, were excluded; second, that there would almost certainly be a General Election shortly. I was abroad during these months, trying to recover my health after a return of trouble due to my war wounds; but I received almost daily bulletins from my wife and my friends about the progress of affairs.

After the Election in the autumn, MacDonald found himself the head of a Coalition which commanded 554 votes in all, including a small number of Liberal Nationals (followers of Simon) and National Labour (followers of MacDonald). Only a few of his Labour Ministers followed him into the new Government, of which the most prominent were Philip Snowden, J. H. Thomas, and the Lord Chancellor, Lord Sankey. Among the less important were Lord de la Warr and his son, Malcolm MacDonald.

His principal adjutant at this time was Philip Snowden. No one could conceive of any two people less alike. Snowden was crippled, always seemed in pain, gallantly struggling against physical disabilities. But he had a character of rare strength and a power of expression quite remarkable. Unlike MacDonald who dealt in broad generalities, he spoke with a clarity and a bitterness which cut through the air like a sword. His sneers were directed upon us for many years; afterwards for a few months they would turn upon his own friends. In the General Election of 1931 they were even more cruel than when they had been used against his own opponents. I never could make out how Snowden had got into the Socialist camp, for his views appeared to be inherited from orthodox and rather old-fashioned Liberalism. His devotion to Free Trade was fanatical. It was not a political device, it was a theological creed. But Snowden had brought into the movement all the real bitterness of the revolutionary. He was not a theorist. He could not be fitted into any of the different classes. He accepted without enthusiasm nationalisation in principle of such things as coal and railways. But at heart he was a Liberal or rather a radical of

Philip Snowden

the old school. Why he joined the Labour movement I do not know, for intellectually he stood a long way above the creed of the nationalisation 'of all the means of production, distribution and exchange'. Outside politics on the few social occasions which I met him he had singular charm. Thin lips which normally gave out such cruel wounding phrases changed into a disarming smile.

Arthur Henderson succeeded to the leadership in 1931. He had come into the movement after the founder. He had been a Liberal agent in the North East and was a true party boss. He understood politics from the inside. He managed the party with an extraordinary skill. He had not the genius of either of his colleagues but much more common sense. Even after the collapse of 1931 Arthur Henderson kept some kind of coherence and discipline among his shattered army. He was a kindly man in his way as all such men are. Although he proved to be a good Foreign Secretary in an impossible position in the second Labour Government, his real talents were political organisation.

I shall try to summarise in another chapter the achievements – and failures – of the National Government, as well as some of the reasons for the collapse of the Labour Government in 1931. MacDonald remained as Prime Minister until June 1935, when he made way for Baldwin. He continued as Lord President for two more years, when he was forced by ill-health to retire.

Whatever may be the criticism of MacDonald's career as a whole, he certainly cannot be lightly dismissed. It was easy, in the last years of his premiership to laugh at the growing 'woolliness' of his thought and speech. Such observations, for instance, as the need to go at a measured pace, 'moving up, up and up, and on, on and on, without experiencing the disastrous effects of sudden breaks in continuity', were really embarrassing for his opponents as well as for his supporters. For the House of Commons is, on the whole, a generous and sympathetic assembly.

But his life must be judged as a whole. He created a great party; he brought it into office for the first time in our history; he repeated this five years later. Although by his decision in 1931 he seemed to destroy his own creation and doom the Labour Party to a long

With Arthur Henderson

eclipse, he acted honourably and in accordance with what he deemed his duty. Those are by no means negligible achievements. Now that the extreme bitterness and rancour caused by the events of 1931 have passed away, it is right to pay tribute to his memory.

CHAPTER FOUR

The National Government

THE birth of the so-called National Government of 1931 constitutes one of the strangest stories in recent political history. The events which led up to the crisis have been the subject of fierce debate. The chief actors have been violently attacked, even traduced, and stoutly defended, then and subsequently. Even now it is hard to paint a fair picture of the personalities involved. It was formed for a specific purpose which was broadly accepted by all parties – that is, the introduction of large economies in order to 'save the pound and restore confidence both at home and abroad'. It was intended that immediately this had been done the uneasy coalition should be dissolved. In fact, in one form or another, it was to continue for nine years. If its last years were a record of weakness, leading to Tragedy, the period before and immediately after its formation, constituted, in the political sense, an episode of High Comedy.

When the Labour Government formed in June 1929 succeeded to Baldwin's long and on the whole successful administration of the last five years, they found the country in a satisfactory condition so far as foreign policy was concerned. The Locarno Treaty of 1925 seemed to have brought some stability into the life of Europe; the Nazi threat was some years away. So far as internal matters were concerned there was economic equilibrium although at a low level of production. All the orthodox plans had been followed with the approbation of the leading politicians and economists, although there were some notable exceptions such as

The Labour Government, 1929

Front row: Clynes, Parmoor, Thomas, Snowden, MacDonald, Henderson, Webb, Sankey, Wedgwood Benn; back row: Lansbury, Alexander, Trevelyan, Bondfield, Thompson, Shaw, Greenwood, Noel Buxton, Graham, Adamson.

Maynard Keynes and the small Conservative group who took their inspiration from him. On the whole, most people accepted the return to gold even at parity with the dollar as a step towards rebuilding the atmosphere and life of the pre-war world. The fact that it made British exports, of which coal was one of the most important, more difficult to sell in foreign markets, had somehow been overlooked. In the same way the heavy industries, iron and steel, engineering, shipbuilding and all the rest were in a state of disarray, with consequently heavy unemployment. But the budget was balanced, the pound stable, and except for the human suffering and economic loss of unused men and machinery the outlook seemed fair enough. Unemployment, when the new Labour Government took over in June 1929, was 1,164,000, a figure which was almost the lowest since 1922 when the post-war boom broke. Moreover so scrupulous was the Treasury that throughout the period of deflation which was necessary to raise the value of the pound and even after that date not only was the budget balanced, but large contributions of some £150 million a year, a further deflationary act, were made by the Sinking Fund in order to reduce the National Debt.

There began a story of rapid deterioration first in America, then in Europe and at home. International trade reached a still lower point. The cessation of large American loans to and investment in Germany revealed the true fact that the Germans had never paid any reparations except by borrowing from America. When this source ceased the German economy began to collapse. All the usual things then started to happen. As the European crisis grew the French bought gold, therefore enormously increasing the difficulties of Great Britain and endangering the whole concept of a free market in currencies. The Bank of England, following its traditional pre-war policy, had borrowed short and lent long; and when the failure of the Creditanstalt Bank produced a panic in Europe the pressures became intolerable. At the same time the Government's expenditure especially on unemployment benefit of various kinds had grown alarmingly. By 31 May 1931 the figure of unemployment had risen to the appalling total of two and a half million. The Chancellor of the Exchequer, Philip Snowden, had agreed in the spring to the appointment of the Geddes Committee whose report at the end of the summer did much to shake public confidence. The strange thing about what followed was the tameness of MacDonald and his colleagues. Some more audacious spirits led by Leo Amery in Parliament and Keynes outside recommended a bolder policy. If given the opportunity they might have challenged altogether the basis of the solution which seemed to be accepted by Labour, Liberals and Conservatives as well as by the great majority of experts in the City and in business. They might have argued that a budget deficit of £170 million, which included the fixed Sinking Fund of £150 million was acceptable. Or if necessary they could have met the shortfall by additional taxation both direct and indirect. They might have closed the increasing gap in the balance of payments by at least a modest tariff for revenue purposes. They might have taken other steps to reduce imports, such as were adopted later in the year; or they might have ventured on a comprehensive system of quotas, import controls, bulk buying and all the rest. In fact the case was never really argued. The Labour Cabinet accepted all the recommenda-

The National Government, 1931
Front row: Snowden, Baldwin, MacDonald, Samuel, Sankey; back row: Cunliffe-Lister, Thomas, Reading, Chamberlain, Hoare.

tions of their orthodox advisers except the small cut in unemployment benefit. On this the Cabinet broke up. Yet it could be argued that although the payments were not generous, in comparison with the then rate of wages and the recent increase in benefits they were by no means contemptible. Moreover their real worth was substantially higher than a few years before owing to the continual fall in prices. The sequel is of course well known. MacDonald, partly because he did not understand economics any more than other people, partly from genuine national feeling and patriotism, partly because he disliked so many of his colleagues, broke up his Government, and a new administration was rapidly constituted. It took office in a strange situation and was itself a strange body. There were ten members, four from the Labour Party, four from the Conservatives and two from the Liberals. The Prime Minister was followed by Snowden, Lord Sankey and

J. H. Thomas. The Conservatives included Baldwin, Hoare, Neville Chamberlain and Cunliffe-Lister. Herbert Samuel, a Liberal, was Home Secretary and Lord Reading, ex-Viceroy of India, ex-Lord Chief Justice, an orthodox Liberal, became Foreign Secretary. Lloyd George was seriously ill; Churchill had separated himself from the Conservative hierarchy. The Government was rapidly formed. It was to save the pound and restore confidence abroad.

However 'the best laid schemes o' mice and men gang aft a-gley'. Happily the British fleet, by following His Majesty's judges in refusing to accept the ten per cent cuts arbitrarily imposed, saved the situation. Panic followed the naval unrest; mutiny was the word generally used, although it was perhaps too harsh. As a result the pound broke and Britain 'went off gold'. Relief was instantaneous, although the situation somewhat bizarre. All the important figures in all the parties, Conservative, Liberal and Labour, had got together with patriotic devotion to save the pound. The Government was formed solely for this purpose and was to come to an end when this purpose was achieved. However, with the relief, like the bursting of an abscess, the body politic seemed almost immediately to show signs of convalescence and the Government proceeded to ask for a dissolution in November. They were returned to power by an overwhelming majority. Yet, in spite of what may be argued in criticism of these curious developments, it is undeniable that the formation of the National Government, with all its imperfections, got us through a dangerous period. Under pressure the Government gradually began to adopt a more expansionist policy. Trade began to revive. Although their introduction involved the resignation of Snowden, tariffs undoubtedly proved of assistance. The Government succeeded in bringing a sense of security and stability in marked contrast to the waffling and wobblings of its predecessor. But the strange thing is that MacDonald and his colleagues, had they shown a little more courage and imagination in 1930 or even in 1931, might have saved themselves and their party. They had the opportunity, but they failed to take advantage of it, largely because they were

# Daily Express

TO-DAY'S WEATHER: Fair.

NO. 9,790.   MONDAY, SEPTEMBER 21, 1931.   ONE PENNY.

BRITAIN OFF THE GOLD STANDARD.

ST NIGHT'S DECISIONS BY THE GOVERNMENT

ISTER running into
on his return from
t for consultations
with the crisis.

No More Gold To Be Sent Abroad.	Stock Exchange Closed To-day.	Bank Rate Up To Six Per Cent.

BUSINESS AS USUAL.

INTERNAL POSITION OF THE COUNTRY IS SOUND."

OVERNMENT announced last night that following the week-end demoralisation of the rnational money market:—

The Gold Standard is suspended from this morning.

The Stock Exchange will not open to-day.

The export of money, except for bona-fide business, will be restricted.

A Bill to give effect to the suspension of the Gold Standard will come before liament to-day.

neously the Bank rate is raised from 4½ to 6 per cent.

ial Stock Exchanges will follow the lead of London and close to-day,

ancellor of the Exchequer will broadcast an explanation of the position from all stations at 9.15 to-night.

GOOD NEWS.

HIS MORNING'S pronouncement from Whitehall is good news.
Nothing more heartening has happened in years.
Never mind how it came about.
Don't waste time in reviling the foreigner or in moaning about the humiliation of events.
The fact remains that at last we are rid of the gold standard—rid of it for good and all.
To future historians it will seem incredible that we should ever have been chained to an arbitrary metal, and that our financial standing in the world should have been at the mercy of unscrupulous and panic-stricken foreign investors.
Now our export trade will have its chance to grow, because the £ will be at its correct level and not an artificially sustained one.
It is true that for a time we shall have to purchase much of our foodstuffs from abroad ; but there is such a surplus of food commodities in the world, and since we are the one great importing country we shall be in the position to protect ourselves against excessive prices.
While we are doing this we can stimulate our own agriculture to the greatest degree, and, by taking our eyes away from New York, from Berlin, from Paris, we can go ahead with plans for a self-sustaining Empire.
We repeat that whatever the difficulties and embarrassments of the moment, this morning's news is good.
It is the end of the gold standard and the beginning of real recovery.

DRAMATIC 'PHONE CALL TO CHEQUERS.

WHY THE PREMIER HURRIED TO LONDON.

FATEFUL MOVES.

FOREIGN ATTACKS ON THE POUND.

" Daily Express " Political Correspondent.

THE events which led up to the dramatic decision of

FRANCE AND U.S. TO HELP THE POUND.

DISCUSSING CREDITS FOR BRITAIN.

"Daily Express" Correspondent.
WASHINGTON,
Sunday, Sept. 20.
Franco-American co-operation to prevent the collapse of sterling will be forthcoming, it is believed in Government circles here.
The Federal Reserve Bank is considering further credits to Great Britain, and, it is understood, is discussing the situation with the Bank of France.
It is expected that the pound can be saved by large additional Franco-American credits which will be arranged shortly.

MISS BONDFIEL ILL.

Miss Margaret Bondfield, Ministe Labour in the last Government, beca suddenly ill during the week-end was removed to a London nur home.
She is suffering from a general vous breakdown, caused by overwo Miss Bondfield is fifty-eight years and at the age of thirteen started a as a teacher in a board school.

LATE NEWS.

---

dominated, even intimidated, by the Treasury and the Chancellor of the Exchequer, Philip Snowden.

Perhaps it is worth recalling, at this point, the story of Sir Oswald Mosley. His Parliamentary career is an outstanding example of the importance of patience in political as well as, perhaps, in other walks of life. Oswald Mosley had been elected after the First War as a Conservative, but soon crossed the floor of the House and joined the Labour Party. He was a good House of Commons speaker, and later became a considerable public orator. He was closely connected with some of the great figures of the old Conservative Party. He had married Lady Cynthia, daughter of Lord Curzon. He was young, handsome and energetic. As soon as the Labour Government of 1929 was formed it was clear that the unemployment problem would be the dominating theme of political controversy. Although the Left-Wing leaders like Wheatley had been conspicuously excluded from the administration and MacDonald's Socialism was beginning to wear pretty thin, Snowden was perhaps an even stronger influence in resisting anything that savoured of Lloyd George's bold expansionist ideas. He wanted peace, retrenchment and reform like the radicals of 1880. However some concession had to be made; so J. H. Thomas – the old railway leader – was put in charge of schemes for employment. He was to be assisted by George Lansbury, the veteran of the party (a sentimental pacifist), Thomas Johnston, the Under-Secretary for Scotland, and young Oswald Mosley. Snowden, of course, made it clear from the start that this body was not to be allowed to be executive or to do anything effective. It was to be advisory. Certainly there were a few minor concessions here and there and a little window-dressing; a number of 'enabling' Acts were accepted by the Treasury watchdogs, but they must not be seriously used.

By June 1930 unemployment had reached two million. (By the summer of 1931 it was to reach 2,700,000.) Meanwhile in the spring of 1930 a document nominally written by Lansbury, Johnston and Mosley, but in fact the composition of the last of these three (and soon to become known and indeed notorious as the 'Mosley Memorandum') had been submitted. This contained a number of expansionist, but not very revolutionary ideas, somewhat on the lines of Lloyd George's proposals. Broadly he asked for planned foreign trade, some public direction of industry, and an expansion policy, financed by public credit. It was rejected by the Cabinet. A month later Mosley resigned. Had he known it, the game was now in his hand. In the meeting of the Labour Party it was clear that the feeling was on his side and against the Ministers. But he made the fatal mistake of insisting upon a vote being taken. When it comes to a vote, loyalty and self-preservation are the dominant forces in party meetings. Had he been content with continuing to work within the party undoubtedly he could have become its leader a year later. For when MacDonald, Snowden, Thomas and all the leading figures appeared to have betrayed the

Sir Oswald Mosley

party, clearly the ordinary Labour member and sympathiser, in and outside the House, would have turned to the only man who had put up any constructive suggestions. MacDonald and his friends, who with the other parties had gone with the so-called National Government, the Labour movement might regard as traitors. But the rest, except for Mosley, what had they done? Month after month they had passively accepted the reactionary views of the Treasury as set forward by Snowden. Here in Mosley the whole party would have found its leader: the man of ideas, the man of courage who alone had faced the realities and tried to bring precise and constructive solutions to the pressing problems of unemployment. Unhappily for him he made the mistake early in 1931, after publishing a manifesto, supported by seventeen other Socialist members including Strachey, Bevan and others, of taking the decisive step of announcing the formation of his New Party. This was a fatal error, and like so many efforts of this kind was doomed to failure.

Since I personally agreed with almost everything in the 'Mosley Memorandum' I naturally got in touch with him, although not now in Parliament. I had only a slight acquaintance with him, although his wife was an old friend of my wife and her family. I had then many conversations with him and was struck by his acute intelligence and energy. Indeed I might have been tempted to join his New Party if I could have seen any practical hope of its success. When I thought it over I realised that traditional political parties are too strongly entrenched to be easily overthrown. It is better for a young man to work within them. The increasing disillusionment with the Labour Government would have given Mosley immense strength inside his own party had he remained. Similarly, in the years to follow, the progressive elements in the Conservative Party were able to make considerable changes in the attitudes of its leader at least in internal and economic affairs. However Mosley not only tried to found a new political party, but when that failed, attempted to change it into a kind of Fascist movement. This, of course, was fatal. As I remember telling him, even if English people felt they faced a crisis and even if they wanted to move into something like overt action, nothing would induce them to put on black shirts and leather belts and march about the streets. They would be more likely to put on their national costume, and hang about Horse Guards in grey flannel trousers and sports jackets, hoping to be allowed to join something.

Mosley's story is really a sad one, something of a tragedy. Great talents and great strength of character were thrown away in vain. Had he waited, he might have been supreme. He struck too soon, and fell for ever. In politics, as in many other things, the essence of the game is 'timing'.

Although as the years passed some of the Conservatives and National Liberal Members, especially those representing the more hard-pressed areas, were critical of the National Government and sometimes exasperated at its apparent inability to deal with the difficulties of their own localities, they were loyal supporters of its general policy. We should have liked more fundamental reforms in certain respects; but we recognised how much was being done. Indeed, modern criticism has not been altogether fair to the achievements of this period. The National Government came into office after a crisis of confidence, in which Britain's credit had sunk to a low level. In the four years of the Parliament our national position had been largely restored. Justice has scarcely been done either to the magnitude of the task or the measure of success. Some recent historians have begun to recognise the facts. 'Re-covery,' C. L. Mowat has written, 'despaired of in 1931, was in the air by 1933, obvious by 1935.' It is true that the Government got little thanks for this improvement. Perhaps the chief reason was that the 'recovery, like the depression, was uneven, so that the misery of the depressed areas drew attention away from the return of prosperity elsewhere. This was the basis for the myth, sedulously propagated later, of the "hungry thirties". The reality was rather different.'

By all ordinary signs, the change was indeed remarkable. From an unfavourable trade balance of £104 million at the beginning of the period, by the end a surplus of £32 million had been earned. The index of production showed that not only had production risen to the 1929 (or pre-crisis) figure, but had passed it by something like ten per cent. The figure of unemployed had been reduced. The total of 1,890,000 in December 1935 was still terrifying; but the movement was in the right direction. Within another year, that is to say in July 1936, it had fallen to 1,600,000.

On the financial and monetary side, the Government used its authority and the confidence which had been created in the world for a mildly expansionist policy. The various cuts in salaries and relief were gradually restored. While Chamberlain resisted the pressure for an unbalanced Budget in 1933, in spite of an agitation for a somewhat more inflationary policy, yet even so the deficit of 1932 was met by borrowing and the Budget of 1933 did not in fact provide for a Sinking Fund.

As I have already recorded, I was one who felt continually impatient, and sought every method of bringing pressure to bear on the leading Ministers. By our various non-party organisations we made perhaps some progress. But Lloyd George terrified Chamberlain (and hated him to the end) and was suspected by Baldwin of every imaginable perfidy. In the event, the electors seemed reasonably satisfied, for in 1935 the National (now almost entirely Conservative) Government was returned to power by a still overwhelming majority.

CHAPTER FIVE

Stanley Baldwin

IN the days about which I am writing the public character of any leading politician seldom bore any close relationship to his true nature. It was largely represented or distorted by party bias, by rumour, and above all by the Press, aided by the caricaturists, among whom were such brilliant examples as Strube and David Low. At least the radio, and especially the television, allow the mass of the public to hear, see and judge the man for themselves. Indeed, with all his faults – its triviality and its superficiality – this medium can be very penetrating. Of all those with whom I was associated or watched from a distance this distortion particularly applied to Stanley Baldwin. He was represented as a Worcestershire squire, whose family had long been engaged both in country affairs and local industry; as a typical Englishman fond of rural life, devoted to his pigs and his garden; and a man of unimaginative but trustworthy solidity, unlike his more mercurial rivals Lloyd George and Churchill. In fact, although he certainly inherited from his father's side this strain in his character, he was endowed from his maternal descent with great imaginative qualities and high idealism. It was not for nothing that his mother was one of the gifted daughters of George Macdonald, one of the great preachers of his day, whose father, James Macdonald, had been ordained by Wesley himself; another of these daughters was the mother of Burne-Jones, another of Rudyard Kipling. These mixed hereditary elements were in fact continually clashing. Thus on the one side, he was sensitive, impulsive, artistic, with a deep know-

ledge of literature and a keen feeling for words; on the other, he
was cautious, and slow. He felt, or at least affected, a certain contempt and fear of any kind of 'brilliance' or even high intelligence.
His bold if rash decision to dissolve the Parliament of 1922, where
he had a sure majority of a hundred or more, in order to hold a sudden
protectionist election in the autumn of 1923 in which he failed to
carry the country, was an example of one side of his nature. So
was his impulsive settlement of the American debt in 1923, when
he was Chancellor of the Exchequer in Bonar Law's Government.
He acted on his own authority and contrary to his instructions.
This was so bitterly resented by his chief that the Prime Minister
threatened to resign and was only persuaded with difficulty to
accept the *fait accompli*. Perhaps also Bonar Law's sense of impending illness may have made him hesitate to break up a Government so recently elected. On the other hand it may be argued that
it was these experiences that made Baldwin so cautious in later years.
At any rate he was not at all the kind of man which he was popularly
believed to be, or that the Conservative Central Office wished in
their propaganda to portray. In 1929 he yielded to the prudent –
even prosaic – side of his nature and was persuaded to adopt the
slogan 'Safety First', with disastrous results. The truth is that like
so many artists – and Baldwin was a true artist – he was subject
to varying moods. At a great crisis he could always rise to meet the
level of events. But after expending the psychological energy
involved there was a reaction; and this led to long periods of
lassitude, inactivity and apparent inability to take decisions or to
face problems.

Baldwin's sensitivity made him shrink from the ordinary
activities of electioneering as they were carried on in those days,
especially in the constituencies. He has described himself how he
regarded as almost degrading the normal routine of working men's
clubs, smoking concerts, comic songs, women's tea-parties and
outings – all of which I personally much enjoyed. Similarly, he
disliked men of genius – a quality which he somehow persuaded
himself was necessarily linked with unreliability, at any rate in
public affairs. Hence his friends were usually mediocre men of

Stanley Baldwin

'A typical Englishman, fond of rural life.'

second-rate parts. He had a particular hatred, amounting almost to an obsession, of Lloyd George, whom he always called 'The Goat'. He disapproved both of his private and his public life. He saw all the faults but seemed to recognise none of the merits. Perhaps it was partly because Lloyd George was a Welshman. Had he been a Worcestershire man or even a Highlander he might have thought differently (yet James Macdonald had married a Welsh girl from the Vale of Clwyd). In return it must be said that Lloyd George always underrated Baldwin. He too did not see beneath the surface. He did not realise that what he took for stupidity was often cunning. Nor did he appreciate the real quality of Baldwin's oratory at its best – based on the old English of *Pilgrim's Progress* or the Psalms. Nobody could have been more relieved at the news of Lloyd George's serious illness at the one moment in his post-war career when he might have returned to power – the crisis of 1931. If Baldwin was sensitive about himself

Speaking on the hustings

he did not always show the same sympathy towards his colleagues. For instance the decision to dissolve the Parliament of 1922 was taken without any consultation with the Cabinet and without notifying those of his colleagues whom he must have known to be, partly by tradition and partly by conviction, inclined to the Free Trade side. These were Lord Derby, Lord Salisbury and the Duke of Devonshire.

If one studies Baldwin's career it is remarkable how these moods of energy and lethargy seemed to follow one another. In the General Strike he showed himself a great statesman, full of sympathetic understanding of the trade unions, and yet firm to resist revolutionary pressure. The Labour leaders knew that he was a man of peace and they themselves wanted to find some excuse to get out of the position into which they had drifted. They remembered his refusal in the previous year, 1925, to accept a Bill calculated to attack what the trade unions regarded as their rights, regarding their political funds. This was the famous speech which ended with the appeal 'Give us peace in our time, O Lord.' I have always believed that it was Baldwin alone who saved the country from a real disaster in 1926. There were some of his colleagues who were more belligerent; but he was, as all the world knew, only carrying out a painful duty and anxious to find an honourable way out.

But after the General Strike was over, he seemed exhausted. He made no effort during the summer (he was, as usual at Aix-les-Bains) to help Churchill's attempt to end the coal strike, which continued dismally month after month. As a result, although the Government of 1924 to 1929 on the whole accomplished much useful and constructive work, it was rejected by the electors. The last two years were sterile, largely because, after the efforts of 1926, the Prime Minister seemed to lose the will or power to govern.

In the House of Commons he was popular with his own party, except perhaps with the extreme Right, and respected and almost loved by the Labour Party. He understood the dangers of the new democracy which had just come into being and tried his best to do two things which he thought vital. First, to divert the Labour Party from extreme Socialist or revolutionary courses, so that it

In Canada with the Duke of Kent and the Prince of Wales

would be able to govern without disaster. Secondly, to educate his own party, as Disraeli had done, to face the new situation. His great predecessor had seen that the Conservatives must be a national party composed of men and women from all walks of life and representing the whole nation. It must be a unifying not divisive force. It must be progressive to face new facts, while retaining all that was best in old traditions. If Baldwin had displayed some real vigour in putting these principles into practice, all would have been well. But he was, after 1926, in an iron-master not a preacher mood.

After his electoral defeat in 1929 Baldwin was violently attacked. Some sections of the party, who should have been his strongest

Lord Rothermere   *Lord Bridgeman*

supporters, were concerned at his apparent apathy. I remember that among the young progressives (the so-called Y.M.C.A., that is my friends and I) many felt that although we would always get a friendly word from him we could get no action. As Lloyd George once said scornfully, 'to try to make any impact on Baldwin was like trying to cut a cushion with a sword'. But the most bitter assaults came from the Right of the party and were led by the powerful Press Lords, Rothermere and Beaverbrook, men of very different character, but both determined to throw out a leader who was responsible for so disastrous a General Election. Rothermere's motive was partly mischief and partly wounded feelings. He resented the fact that he could not play the same sort of role as his brother Northcliffe had played during the war and after. Beaverbrook was inspired by his life-long determination to realise Joseph Chamberlain's dream of an imperial *Zollverein*; or as he now called it, Empire Free Trade. In one of his dark moods Baldwin was ready to yield to the pressure. Indeed it was only by the persuasion of his devoted friend Willy Bridgeman that he roused himself to fight. This was during the famous by-election in the St George's constituency in London where Duff Cooper soundly defeated the Beaverbrook–Rothermere candidate, and where Lady

Duff Cooper and Lady Diana at the St George's by-election

Diana reproduced in another century the charms by which
Georgiana, Duchess of Devonshire had won over the rough electors
of Westminster to the support of Fox. For once in his life Baldwin
became angry. The culminating point of a famous speech that he
gave at this time is a sentence that will live in political history.
He turned upon the two Press Lords, who never spoke in Parliament
but used Fleet Street not Westminster as their base. 'What the
proprietorship of these papers is aiming at is power, and power
without responsibility – the prerogative of the harlot throughout

the ages.' Before this by-election almost every leading Conservative agreed that Baldwin must go. After it, in June 1930, he had no difficulty of carrying by a large majority meetings of the party, Members and candidates. Here again he was much assisted by his enemies; for he was able to quote with considerable effect, a letter from Rothermere to a Conservative Member. The great newspaper magnate had impudently demanded not only to know what the policy would be at the next election but to be supplied with the names of Baldwin's most prominent colleagues in the next Ministry if he were to win. This insolence the whole party deeply resented. After his triumph in the summer of 1930 Baldwin relapsed into quiet again. He took little part in the crisis that led up to the formation of the National Government in 1931. Immediately after the end of the session he had gone to Aix-les-Bains with his wife for the long rest to which he felt entitled. Somebody bitterly observed that it was not Worcestershire but Aix-les-Bains that was his true spiritual home. In any case, he left it all to Neville Chamberlain and his colleagues; only with great difficulty was he brought back to London. He acquiesced happily in serving under Ramsay MacDonald as Lord President in the National Government, and took little part in subsequent events except to do everything he could to oppose Lloyd George's New Deal proposals, admirable as they were and soundly based upon expert knowledge and opinion; and also, more constructively, to support Halifax's policy on India. The office of second-in-command to MacDonald suited him admirably. Poor Bonar Law had spent the war in restraining a dynamic Prime Minister. MacDonald was not so fatiguing.

Baldwin drifted happily along until 1935 when it was clear that MacDonald, who was now decaying in body and mind, could not continue. Just before the Election of 1935 Baldwin became Prime Minister. Had he also decided to retire from public life at this date he would have gone down to history as one of the great British statesmen, at any rate so far as the conduct of home affairs was concerned. He had saved us from something like revolution at the time of a national strike, a crisis which if badly handled might

The Abdication—a lone demonstrator in Downing Street

have led to disaster. He had imposed upon the Conservative Party concepts of what its character and structure should be. While he had disappointed some of the more eager spirits, young men like my friends and myself, he had earned our respect and affection. But the years of his premiership, 1935 to 1937, with one exception proved disastrous. That exception was, of course, the Abdication crisis. No man could have handled it more tenderly or with greater dignity. To him therefore both the Crown and the Commonwealth owe a lasting debt. But in every other respect he was out of touch with the rapid movement of events. Having no personal experience of the fighting services – he was too old for the First War – he failed altogether to understand the character of modern armaments, especially the new and more sophisticated weapons. He had had nothing to do with the making of munitions; he had never served either as a subordinate or chief Minister in any of the service departments; he had studied neither tactics and strategy (as Churchill had), nor the preparation for war. Thus when a programme of rearmament was finally and tardily approved it was a slow-motion affair. The appointment of Sir Thomas Inskip, an agreeable but not brilliant lawyer, as Minister for the Co-ordination of Defence showed that Baldwin had no comprehension of the defence problem. Without a staff, without a directive and without any authority, no Minister could possibly succeed.

At the same time he regarded foreign affairs with such distaste that he neglected what is really the first duty of a Prime Minister – close co-operation with the Foreign Secretary and a perpetual watch on the foreign situation. If this is true today, it was still more true in Baldwin's time when Britain and the British Empire stood as one of the most powerful organisations in the world. He left foreign affairs to the Foreign Ministers, and during this period they were for the most part weak or ineffective. Even Eden, who was appointed in December 1935, after Hoare's dismissal, could get very little help from Baldwin. On one point his memory has been vindicated. By a misunderstanding of a famous speech, by which he seemed to admit sacrificing the safety of the nation to political advantage, he was bitterly criticised during and after the war. Even his first biographer, G. M. Young, attempted no defence. It is a strange, and characteristic episode. Baldwin's merits as an orator consisted of his ability to speak without a text and often really from the heart. (When he used a text, the speech was generally weak, sometimes painful.) But this method has its risks. For instance, when the first news broke of the famous – or infamous – Hoare–Laval agreement in Paris for the partitioning of Abyssinia a few weeks after a General Election fought and won on the opposite policy, Baldwin, now Prime Minister, had to face a very hostile

House of Commons. His latest biographers, Keith Middlemas and John Barnes, have described the affair:

The debate in the House was disastrous. Baldwin attempted to finesse the Opposition by reference to hidden truths, a tactic which comes easier to a politician accustomed to duplicity. He told the House that it was premature to disclose anything until the matter had been before the League and the parties concerned. His lips were 'not yet unsealed'; but when these troubles were past he could make a case and 'guarantee that not a Member would go into the Lobby against us'. In a disconsolate speech it was, as he admitted after, 'one of the stupidest things I ever said'. For months David Low, the cartoonist, never drew him without sticking plaster across his mouth. The gambit failed. Baldwin had spoken bitterly of leaks and inaccuracies; the Opposition were not slow to point out that, even if the newspaper reports were only partly correct, they still revealed the abandonment of the policy on which the Government had fought the election.

Similarly, on an even more vital issue, rearmament. On 12 November 1936 Churchill had delivered a powerful philippic, which deeply impressed the whole House and especially affected the Conservatives, already angered by the Inskip appointment. After reproaching the Government for their failures, he ended with these words, 'The Government cannot make up their minds, or they cannot get the Prime Minister to make up his mind. So they go on, in strange paradox, decided only to be undecided, resolved to be irresolute, adamant for drift, solid for fluidity, all-powerful to be impotent. So we go on, preparing more months and years – precious, perhaps vital – for the locusts to eat.' The last phrase was to become famous. In reply, Baldwin, speaking partly from a text, but partly from rough notes, did his best. But unhappily it was one of those pieces of almost 'thinking aloud' which were often very effective and endeared him to the House; this time it failed. He tried to explain the difficulties of democratic government and the importance of timing. What he meant to say was that in 1933 it would not have been possible to start rearmament on a big scale or to have won an Election *at that time* on such a proposal. What he appeared to say was that the 1935 Election could not have been won on a strong rearmament policy and that therefore Baldwin had, in Churchill's cruel words in his own memoirs, 'put party before country'. The answer, as set out by Baldwin's defenders, is satisfactory. It is clear, if the speech is carefully studied, that Baldwin had in mind the impossibility at the time of the Fulham by-election (the disastrous loss of a safe Conservative seat) and the Peace Ballot, of risking an Election in 1933 or 1934.

The Peace Ballot was one of those strange episodes which made a vast impact on contemporary politics and is now, no doubt, completely forgotten. It was organised by the League of Nations Union (an all-party British society formed to support the principle of the League; its most powerful leader was Lord Robert Cecil). This body organised not a 'sample' on the model of Gallup and other so-called 'polls' but a house-to-house canvass of the whole nation. The questions were skilfully phrased and the response was enormous. Carefully studied it was a vote for the League.

Of $11\frac{1}{2}$ million replies, all answered the first four questions as the promoters hoped. The last was more tricky. Should an aggressor be stopped by 'sanctions', such as a trade blockade, or in the last resort by war? $6\frac{1}{4}$ million answered yes. But how was this 'collective security' to operate? Who would contribute and how much? On this vital issue there was a discreet silence. As a result, although strictly interpreted, the replies were reasonably robust, the general inference was ambivalent. It was certainly no basis for a rearmament campaign, which was soon to become desperately urgent.

Nevertheless, even in 1935 the issue was not very clearly put. It was no clarion call. Certainly, Baldwin asked for powers to rearm. But his appeal to the nation was somewhat equivocal. He roared like any sucking dove. The people were not given the true picture; at the same time it is doubtful whether the Government itself realised the extent of the danger. In any case, the charge of deliberately postponing the necessary rearmament measures so as to win the 1935 Election is not correct. Baldwin's own words (as in the case of Abyssinia) were partly responsible for the confusion.

Naturally, when disaster came upon us, especially after the terrible days of 1940, it was convenient for many people who had

'*Off for the holidays*': *cartoon by David Low, 31 July 1936*

Left to right: Inskip, Simon, Cunliffe-Lister, Cooper, Hoare, Chamberlain, Baldwin, Eden

not themselves been conspicuous supporters of rearmament or a strong foreign policy to turn upon the unhappy Baldwin, now living in retirement, and put all the blame upon him. Among the many cruel episodes was the mean refusal of the County Council, confirmed by the Minister of Works, to spare from the scrap collection the gates in his park and garden. Only the ornamental gates presented to him in 1937 were left in place. The question was mishandled; Baldwin's appeal was made the occasion for vile and wicked attacks, in the Press and in Parliament, by men who were themselves contemptible. One, who should have known better, was Lord Beaverbrook, who might have helped to prevent this outrage.

The worst offenders were the extreme Left-Wing authors of such books as *Guilty Men*, who were far more guilty themselves. From this extreme and unfair criticism Baldwin's memory has now been rescued. Nevertheless it is a weakness, an undeniable weakness in his career, that he seemed to have such blind spots.

The truth is that, like many other people, he could not believe that there could be a man in the world so wicked and so lacking in any kind of moral feeling as Hitler. Baldwin's life had been cast on the whole in pleasant places. He had had to deal with a lot of people with varying degrees of good and evil in their character. He attributed certainly some Mephistophelian characteristics to Lloyd George, but that was only half serious. He had never believed that there could be a living devil, so although the full development of Hitler's career came after his resignation he was unable to attune his mind to the thought that in this century of 'progress' the world might be hurled for a second time into the abyss of destructive war.

Baldwin was, therefore, a great Peace Minister, in many ways comparable to Walpole, whom he much admired. He had the same common sense and the same love of England. Although altogether different in his private character – as far apart as possible – he had the same power of managing men by a simple, direct speech, eschewing the elaborate rhetorical fashions of his day. Similarly, while Baldwin's oratory could not compare with the dynamic force of Lloyd George or Churchill, it suited the popular taste better – at least in quiet times. In addition, he was a master of the simple, but practical, themes which touched many springs in English hearts and memories. Two passages, quoted by G. M. Young, are worth recalling. The first, in 1925, is part of an address to the Classical Association. After speaking of the value of the Greek and Roman heritage, he ended with a passage which is typical of him at his best:

At the microphone in 1924

I remember many years ago standing on the terrace of a beautiful villa near Florence. It was a September evening, and the valley below was transfigured in the long horizontal rays of the declining sun. And then I heard a bell, such a bell as never was on land or sea, a bell whose every vibration found an echo in my innermost heart. I said to my hostess, 'that is the most beautiful bell I have ever heard'. 'Yes,' she replied, 'it is an English bell.' And so it was. For generations its sound had gone out over English fields, giving the hours of work and prayer to English folk from the tower of an English abbey, and then came the Reformation, and some wise Italian bought the bell whose work at home was done and sent it to the Valley of the Arno, where after four centuries it stirred the heart of a wandering Englishman and made him sick for home. Thus the chance word of a Latin inscription, a line in the Anthology, a phrase of Horace or a 'chorus ending of Euripides', plucks at the heartstrings and stirs a thousand memories, memories subconscious and ancestral.

On a quite different occasion, faced with the difficult task of paying tribute to a great Parliamentary figure, Austen Chamberlain, he moved the House by the sincerity and simplicity of his words.

In . . . that countryside where I was born and where old English phrases linger . . . even now I hear among those old people this phrase about those who die: 'He has gone home.' It was a universal phrase among the old agricultural labourers, whose life was one toil from their earliest days to the last, and I think it must have arisen from the sense that one day the toil would be over and the rest would come, and that rest would be home. So they say 'He has gone home'.

When our long days of work are over here there is nothing in our oldest customs which so stirs the imagination of the young Member as the cry which goes down the Lobbies: 'Who goes home?' Sometimes when I hear it, I think of the language of my countryside, feeling that for those who have borne the almost insupportable burden of public life there may well be a day when they will be glad to go home. So Austen Chamberlain has gone home . . . the best thing we can do to honour his memory is to cling more closely to the two things to which he clung throughout his life. He always maintained that public service was the highest career a man could take . . . He had an infinite faith in the Parliamentary system of this country. Let us resolve once more that we can best keep his memory bright by confirming our own resolution that government of the people by the people shall never perish on the earth.

For many years it has been the fashion to denigrate Baldwin's memory. That was perhaps natural during and after the years of storm and stress. Today, when we are suffering not from external menaces so much as from internal strife, when so many of our wounds are self-inflicted, we may wish that the influence of such a man were once again exerted in the cause of peace and unity.

CHAPTER SIX

Neville Chamberlain

WHAT an extraordinary, almost unique family. They were all Victorians. Iain Macleod has written, 'Neville Chamberlain, the youngest of them was already in his thirties when Queen Victoria died. And they represented a new and important element in the Conservative Party, the well-to-do middle class. They were men of property. They were as solid as their silver.' But of course they were not, and never became Tories. Joseph Chamberlain, the head of the great clan, was not only a Liberal, but a Radical – many, including the old Queen, thought him a dangerous agitator. Mr Gladstone feared and rather disliked him. Had it not been for Gladstone's sudden conversion to Home Rule for Ireland in 1886, Joseph Chamberlain would have remained in the Liberal Party, and have made a bold bid for its leadership.

The schism of 1886 proved a watershed in modern politics. It was not, perhaps, surprising that the Whigs could not stomach the old man's sudden twists of policy. For, in many respects, they had long been uneasy. But that Joseph Chamberlain, the great radical leader, should found a new party and bring it into alliance with Lord Salisbury and the Tories was indeed a portent. For 'our Joe', as Birmingham knew him, had moved, to use modern parlance, far to the Left. The 'unauthorised programme' which he put forward in 1885 had deeply shocked Gladstone, partly because it was radical and partly because it was unauthorised. Moreover, he was a Unitarian (which was displeasing to Gladstone's High Church traditionalism); he was a provincial, a Lord Mayor, who

The Chamberlain family

had not only urged but brought about in the city which he governed such novelties as municipal banking and other far-reaching schemes of municipal undertakings.

I never saw the great man, for in 1906, just after the General Election which destroyed his grand imperial design, he was struck down by paralysis. He lived on for eight painful years – his mind as strong as ever, his body useless. But I can well remember, during the Boer War and after, when 'Joe', with his monocle, his orchid, his immaculate dress, his commanding personality, was a national hero. Some, of course, hated him and all his works; others admired him and almost worshipped him. None could underrate his dynamic power, his administrative genius, and his talents both in Parliament and on the platform. But few could resist that combination of charm and strength, which made even his old Liberal colleagues remain on friendly terms in private during the bitter years of 1889 to 1901. John Morley, his closest colleague in the radical days, preserved a deep affection for his old friend.

Austen Chamberlain, Joseph's eldest son, was a man of very different stamp. He looked very like his father, and cultivated the resemblance, monocle and all. Austen's mother died at his birth – and by a tragic fatality Neville's mother, Joseph's second wife, was also to die in childbirth. So Austen was brought up in the famous Highbury circle, listening from a child to grand talk, political and literary, among a group of men of high quality. He went early into politics, and spent his long life as a member of the House of Commons. He achieved high office – Chancellor of the Exchequer, Foreign Secretary. His greatest triumph was Locarno – a treaty which seemed (alas, illusory hope) to bring real peace to Europe. But Austen was, except in appearance, very unlike his father. He spoke well, but never in the grand style. He was clear, but not incisive. He was loved by all for his courtesy and his sweetness of character, as well as for his high sense of loyalty. There was not really much of Birmingham about him; sometimes he almost seemed a *grand seigneur*. He was respected, but never feared. He had two opportunities of perhaps seizing the leadership. On each occasion his sense of honour and loyalty held him back. It was said of him, cynically, that 'Austen always played the game; and always lost.'

His half-brother, Neville, was perhaps nearer to his father in character and modes of thought. He had something of the clear, incisive, and often bitter qualities in his speeches which had made

Joseph Chamberlain   *Austen Chamberlain*

Joseph feared. But he had little of the warmth that made his father loved. Somehow it was all on a lower note. He was effective in speech but never overwhelming. He excelled in clear exposition but he seldom rose to anything like emotion. The only occasion which I can remember when his true sentiments seemed to break through was when he introduced in the first years of the National Government a new tariff system and referred to the last campaign which had brought his father glory, but defeat – and at a bitter cost.

After an unfortunate five years in the Bahamas, as the manager of an enterprise which had struck the imagination of his father, Neville returned home to Birmingham in 1896. That adventure was formally wound up in 1897. It was an unlucky speculation. The father lost a sum of at least £50,000; the son had the mortification of watching a bold adventure come to nothing, yet through no fault of his own. It is a tribute to his stamina that he recovered from this experience and threw himself into business and municipal politics with enthusiasm. He bought and managed a small company called Hoskins; he went on the boards of some larger undertakings; he embarked on municipal life, with all that this implied in Birmingham regarding national politics. He became Lord Mayor.

He threw himself, like his father, into the clearing of slums, building of hospitals and many similar social reforms. If, as part of his alliance with the Conservatives and to defend the integrity of the United Kingdom, 'Joe' had seen many (but not all) of his reforming visions evaporate, Neville was able to carry on the tradition in the municipal sphere.

During the First War, Neville had another frustrating experience, not so long, but almost as painful as he had suffered in the West Indies. By the end of 1916, soon after Lloyd George had succeeded to Asquith, he found the manpower situation chaotic. His remedy was to appoint a Director-General of National Service in charge both of the military and the civil side of universal national service. There were, of course, two distinct branches, each under their own director, both responsible to the Director-General. This post, after it had been offered to one or two politicians who were too fly to enter on so difficult a task with such undefined powers, Neville agreed to accept. But unluckily for him, another organisation, this time a proper Ministry with all its apparatus, was also being formed – the Ministry of Labour. The responsibilities of this Ministry and Neville's rather inchoate organisation naturally clashed. Without going into details which would now be wearisome, Neville failed – partly from ignorance of Whitehall, partly from inexperience of politics and Lloyd George's often unconventional methods, and within six months he resigned. He had made some valuable and important contributions to the problem, as was later acknowledged. But he had failed. His successor, Sir Auckland Geddes, had advantages denied to Neville. He was an M.P., the head of a regular department, and of Cabinet rank. He wisely demanded, and obtained, a clear directive; he became a member of the Committee of the War Cabinet over which Smuts presided. Poor Neville was thrown into a confused tangle without any of these advantages. He must sometimes have thought that he was back in the Bahamas. The most lasting, and perhaps the most regrettable, result of this episode was a distrust of Lloyd George which could easily be stimulated by Baldwin from distaste to animosity.

Neville's career, after this unhappy setback, was a series of successes. He was elected as member for the Ladywood division of Birmingham in 1918. Such was the loyalty which 'Joe's' memory commanded and so powerful the machine – the famous Caucus – which had been created, that all twelve Birmingham seats were won. Although he made his mark early in the House of Commons, he could scarcely hope for office under Lloyd George after the calamity of 1917. When the coalition fell, he was offered the place of Postmaster-General by Bonar Law, which he accepted, in spite of his natural loyalty to his brother Austen, who had gone out of office with Lloyd George. From that moment his political career went forward easily and without any mishap, or even hitch. His career as Minister of Health began in March 1923. It was interrupted by a few months as Chancellor of the Exchequer following Bonar Law's resignation, and by the short Labour Government of 1923 to 1924. Then for four or five years he carried out as Minister of Health all the tasks which he had set himself.

His years as Minister of Health from 1924 to 1929 were probably the happiest in his life. He was popularly supposed to have compiled, in the first few weeks, a list of all the Bills he intended to carry through the Parliament. They numbered a score or more, and included such vast schemes as Poor Law reform, local government reorganisation, widows and orphans pensions, as well as measures for planning, housing, and slum clearance and the like. Before the Parliament ended, he was able to tick the last one off the list. In any event, he had proved himself one of the great reformers – not in words or promises, but in deeds and performance. Those who today only think of Neville Chamberlain in connection with Munich and the tragic years of his premiership, should not, in justice, forget this splendid period of solid achievement.

In the 1931 crisis, and the events which led to the formation of the National Government, he took the leading part. Baldwin was abroad; Churchill was separated from the hierarchy of the party. After the General Election in November 1931 (which he urged with all his energy on a reluctant MacDonald), he became all-powerful in the economic and financial field. His Budgets gradually became more expansionist as the pound recovered and the nation seemed to be in better heart. But he resisted with all his native obstinacy any attempt even to understand, still less to adopt, Lloyd George's 'New Deal'. He continued, through the Abyssinian crisis, through the early Hitler acts of aggression (such as the remilitarisation of the Rhineland) to accept the situation, without perhaps fully understanding its implications. During the last years of the partnership between MacDonald and Baldwin he was the strongest figure in the Government, if and when he chose to exert his will. While MacDonald was incoherent and Baldwin dilatory, Neville Chamberlain was the most effective Minister and the most active.

If Baldwin's place in history would have been far higher had he retired from office at the same time as MacDonald – in 1935 – it is equally true that Neville Chamberlain, had he never become Prime Minister for those three fatal years, would have been remembered only as one of the most progressive and effective social reformers of his own or almost any time. Certainly the two men were of very different stamp. Baldwin was lethargic, imaginative, uncertain of himself, the artist in politics. Neville Chamberlain was full of energy and was quite sure of himself. In his earlier days his undoubted intellectual arrogance was partly concealed. After he became Prime Minister, and especially after Munich, it developed almost to a form of mania. Yet at all times he was a difficult man to argue with. Thus in debate he was seldom conciliatory and generally unyielding. He knew he was right on every question. Baldwin was never quite sure that anybody was right, especially himself. Baldwin's approach to problems was largely one of temperament and feeling. Chamberlain brought to them a clear, logical and sometimes ruthless mind. Nor did he take any trouble to make himself agreeable even to his supporters, still less to his opponents. He seldom if ever came into the Smoking Room or joined in the camaraderie of the House of Commons. He was, in Dr Johnson's phrase, an 'unclubbable' man.

In Parliament, as in Council, the two men were of very opposing

Chamberlain as Chancellor on Budget Day 1936

types. Baldwin was conciliatory and popular in all parts of the House. The Labour Members, especially the genuine trade union Members of whom we had then a large number (they are now mostly university-trained intellectuals) felt a real affection for him. He understood them and they understood him. They knew the problems of industry from their side and he knew them from the managerial side; but not the problems of the vast and rather faceless industries which, whether nationalised or still privately controlled, have largely taken the place of the old family firms. Chamberlain, in spite of his Birmingham experience, seemed to have forgotten or been perhaps too reserved to show any sympathy for or understanding of ordinary, or stupid, men. Baldwin had warned him of this in 1927. Chamberlain, in Iain Macleod's words, 'always gave the impression that he looked on the Labour Party as dirt. The impression was shared by the Labour Party.'

I first met him in the Parliament of 1924 to 1929. Even then he was a somewhat forbidding figure. He had a sardonic, not to say contemptuous, look and spoke with a harsh and rasping voice. Curiously enough with his fine features he reminded one more of a crow than of an eagle. And that tiny pin-head – what did that imply? Efficiency, perhaps, but not genius. I also used to meet him fairly frequently socially either in London or in the country. He was a particularly welcome guest at the Astors' at Cliveden, where my wife and I went very often. (Nancy Astor was devoted to Dorothy, and the affection was mutual.) Even in the country he had a curiously stiff appearance, like those old daguerreotypes of the host's father or grandfather which hung about in the passages and gun-rooms of country houses.

On the other hand once you got to know him he could exercise considerable charm. Indeed I began soon to realise that underneath his stern exterior was at any rate in those days a warm and even sentimental heart. I was perhaps influenced by a special act of kindness at the beginning of my political life. Some of my friends and I published a little book in 1927, and he not only read it and sent a congratulatory letter, but also included three pages of closely typed foolscap dealing one by one with our proposals. That from a Cabinet Minister to a newly elected Member was worth a great deal. A few fulsome phrases can be dashed off by a private secretary and signed by his chief but an elaborate critique of a book was a real compliment. I had some discussion and even clash with him at later stages of this Parliament, in particular with regard to the proposals for the de-rating of industry. He obviously disliked my venturing to act as a kind of emissary of Churchill. He was clearly shocked that any private Member should take part in the formulation of policy, or be admitted to any confidences.

Both in the Parliament of 1924 to 1929 and still more after 1930 when Churchill had retired like Achilles to his tent, he dominated the Conservative Party and to a large extent the Parliament. In 1930 to 1931 he was loyal to Baldwin, whom he might have destroyed for his own benefit. He clearly resented Baldwin's indolence, but this never led him to fall into the temptation of trying to supersede him. This was partly from real genuine goodness of heart and partly from a certain shrewdness. He knew that no Zimri is likely to have peace after he has slain his master. Only in times of grave emergency, like war, is Omri's murder pardonable; even then it rankles with Omri's relations and friends. But it always fell to Chamberlain to do all the work. During the crisis of 1931 Chamberlain had to act in Whitehall while Stanley Baldwin and Lucy were resting in Haute Savoie. With great difficulty Baldwin was persuaded to come back, but only for a day or two. Chamberlain in fact took charge of the negotiations especially those regarding the personalities of the National Government, a matter always distasteful to Baldwin. It was he who forced the pace leading to the General Election in the autumn of 1931 and it was really he who took the lead in trying to persuade MacDonald and Baldwin to face some of the realities. It should not be forgotten that so far as any rearmament was embarked upon in the following years it was largely due to Chamberlain's pressure.

Then at last, in 1937, after the coronation of George VI, the old Prime Minister retired, full of years and to the sound of universal praise and acclamation; soon, such is the fickleness of fate, to be turned to snarls of recrimination and almost hatred. There was no question of election or the new nonsense of 'the magic circle'. Chamberlain succeeded inevitably, just as Anthony Eden succeeded Churchill. There could be no other choice.

Yet it was a fatal decision both for him and his country; and, alas, for Europe.

There is nothing so difficult or delicate in the management of a government as the relations between the Prime Minister and the Foreign Secretary. They must really be like brothers in a partnership. They must meet frequently, almost every day, especially in this period, when Britain and the British Empire stood in potential strength and actual authority equal to any of the great nations of the world. Both sides of Downing Street must work in complete harmony if confusion and something worse are to be avoided. But Chamberlain, who had never served in the army, who had never played in a team (except perhaps the family team) had always been a masterful figure in any organisation in which he worked. He either did not understand or wilfully set aside even the outward forms of loyalty to his Foreign Secretary. Samuel Hoare (afterwards Lord Templewood) has vividly described in a very fair volume of reminiscences the curious method by which Chamberlain conducted foreign affairs after he succeeded in ousting Anthony Eden. In the chapter entitled 'The Big Four' Hoare throws, perhaps unconsciously, a powerful but sinister light upon this strange system. The 'Big Four' consisted of Chamberlain, the Prime Minister; Halifax the Foreign Secretary; Sir John Simon, now Chancellor of the Exchequer; and Sam Hoare, now Home Secretary. According to Hoare the officials attending were Sir Alec Cadogan, the head of the Foreign Office; Sir Robert Vansittart, the former head of the Foreign Office who had been elevated to a position of nominally greater importance but actual impotence; and curiously enough Sir Horace Wilson, who although he had no knowledge or experience of foreign affairs, was head of the civil service and known to be the Prime Minister's *éminence grise*. This was a curious way to do business. Of course, during my Premiership, the Foreign Secretary and I would often invite to a specially-called meeting Ministers and officials from other departments to consider some particular and pressing problem. But I never allowed anything like what Hoare calls (and clearly revels in) the Big Four to come into existence. Indeed I

Chamberlain and Hoare *Vansittart and Cadogan*

remember once an idea which was strongly held in Whitehall that the Foreign Office buildings were obsolete and should be pulled down. An ambitious plan was devised to seize Carlton House Terrace and other adjacent buildings for the new Foreign Office. I absolutely declined to allow it to proceed. This was not on the question of design or expense or any such mundane considerations. My objection was simply this. The Foreign Secretary, I insisted, must be within walking distance of the Prime Minister, just as the Chancellor of the Exchequer lives in an adjoining house. If he is at Carlton House Terrace, it means one private secretary ringing up another to make an appointment. If he is across the road he just steps in, morning or afternoon, for a glass of sherry and a chat at least every other day. No formal meetings can replace that intimacy. But this was not Chamberlain's idea at all. His first Foreign Secretary, Anthony Eden, was Baldwin's appointment. Chamberlain found him already in place. The two men were very unsympathetic. Nor had Chamberlain much use for the Foreign

Office officials and their methods. There was a little of the old
middle-class suspicion of the aristocratic idlers who had filled
the saloons and corridors of the Foreign Office. This, of course,
was mere prejudice; for few were aristocratic, and none idle.

The story of 1937 to 1940, of Chamberlain's short career at the
head of affairs, has often been told, and it is a tragic one. It has
been his fate, as so often with statesmen, to be at first obsequiously
praised then extravagantly abused. Unhappily for himself and his
country he seemed to have been possessed by some kind of mystical
spirit. When he took office, disregarding all advice and warnings
until it was too late, he still believed in his own mission to save
and secure the peace of the world. This he pursued with almost
fanatical determination until the bitter moment in March 1939
when Hitler marched into Prague. Even then he could scarcely
believe that he had been betrayed. He thought apparently of the
dictators as if they were foreign business men with whom, either
as a business man or as Lord Mayor of Birmingham, he was doing
some deal. They might haggle a bit, but if they settled, they would
keep to their bargain. He did not conceive that there could be
such a man as Hitler, absolutely ruthless and quite regardless of
any promises or pledged word. Yet, after all, what was Hitler but
an exaggerated Bismarck? Even if his was almost a caricature of
the old Prussian system, it was the same idea. One could forge a
telegram, the other break a pledge or a treaty without turning a
hair. Baldwin suffered from the same illusions. Perhaps neither
believed in original sin.

In any event, all this world was new to Chamberlain, outside
his ken. So he first drove Anthony Eden to resignation by acts of
disloyalty which are scarcely believable, but are strangely enough
admitted in his own diary, where he noted: 'I wrote a letter to
Mussolini in friendly terms and this was followed by a very cordial
reply from him. I did not show my letter to the Foreign Secretary,
for I had the feeling that he would object to it.' Then with his
Foreign Secretary in the House of Lords, the charming, urbane
but essentially pliable Halifax, he took effective control. The
tragic story then unfolds itself with all the inevitability of a Greek

Lord Halifax

drama. The unhappy Prime Minister is at once the centre and the victim of the dreadful story now so well known to us. But again we must be fair. Although as members of the Cabinet, both Chamberlain and Eden were partly responsible, or at least collectively responsible, for the weakness in British armaments, yet it is hard to put all the blame upon Baldwin or his successors. The whole spirit of the country was then deeply pacifist. The so-called 'Peace Ballot' organised by Lord Cecil and his friends had resulted in a strangely confused vote. But the general impression was that of opposition to force. It is true that 'collective force' would be all right in certain cases; but whence it was to be obtained was obscure. What collective force was there? In the League of Nations? But the League of Nations was only the sum of its members. The United States did not belong. The position of Russia was doubtful. The Germans had left. All the British forces were under-manned and under-armed. The French Air Force was notoriously weak. Italy was against the League even before the Abyssinian adventure, for dictators don't like these organisations. From where then was this collective security to come? It is said that a chain is only as strong as its weakest link; but in the poor League of Nations all the links were weak and dropping out one by one. The Liberal and Labour Parties consistently opposed, right up to the edge of war, both conscription and effective rearmament. A clever propaganda movement after the war persuaded the public that the fault all lay with Baldwin and Chamberlain. Alas, the fault lay not in the stars, but in ourselves – in the Parliamentary and democratic system itself.

Whatever Chamberlain's faults, he did not lack courage. Few people today, when we all hop about the world in package tours without turning a hair, realise what were the conditions of flying nearly forty years ago. For an old gentleman of seventy, who had never been in the air, to make these journeys in the machines then available was a very serious undertaking. He did not shrink from the ordeal. Nor did he find any difficulty in subsequent months in justifying and glorying in his work. Moreover he was supported after Munich by an almost unanimous nation giving vociferous

DAILY
SKETCH

No. 9,177   SATURDAY, OCTOBER 1, 1938   ONE PENNY

PEACE
SOUVENIR
ISSUE
WIRELESS: P. 19

PREMIER SAYS 'PEACE FOR OUR TIME'—P. 3

Give Thanks In Church To-morrow

TO-MORROW is Peace Sunday.

Hardly more than a few hours ago it seemed as if it would have been the first Sunday of the most senseless and savage war in history.

The "Daily Sketch" suggests that the Nation should attend church to-morrow and give thanks.

THE fathers and mothers who might have lost their sons, the young people who would have paid the cost of war with their lives, the children who have been spared the horror of modern warfare—let them all attend Divine Service and kneel in humility and thankfulness.

To-morrow should not be allowed to pass without a sincere and reverent recognition of its significance.

MR. CHAMBERLAIN SHOWS THE PACT AT HESTON

'Never To Go To War Again'

WHEN Mr. Chamberlain arrived at Heston last night he said:

"This morning I had another talk with the German Chancellor, Herr Hitler. Here is a paper which bears his name as well as mine. I would like to read it to you:

"'We, the German Fuehrer and Chancellor and the British Prime Minister, have had a further meeting to-day and are agreed in recognising that the question of Anglo-German relations is of the first importance for the two countries and for Europe.

"'We regard the agreement signed last night and the Anglo-German Naval Agreement as symbolic of the desire of our two peoples never to go to war with one another again.

"'We are resolved that the method of consultation shall be the method adopted to deal with any other questions that may concern our two countries and we are determined to continue our efforts to remove possible sources of difference and thus to contribute to the assurance of peace in Europe.'"

(Here are the signatures on the pact)

September 30, 1938.

applause whenever he appeared, regarding him as the saint who had come on earth to save them and their children from the horrors of war. Even in the House of Commons the attacks of the Opposition were at first somewhat muted, because he could always reply that it was they who had refused to provide Britain with strong armaments, the essential instruments of strong diplomacy. His critics on the Conservative side, led by Churchill and Eden, were much more outspoken, but they were very few. I think that in the first few weeks after the agreement of Munich in 1938 there were not more than twenty or thirty of us who dissented from the general chorus of approval. But as the winter passed and the constant repetition of the word 'appeasement' began to sound like a dirge rung by a cracked church bell, feelings began to change. Hitler's demands were not appeased. The appetite grew with what it fed on; and in the end poor Chamberlain had to see his whole policy collapse. He had to lead his Government to a declaration of a war which he had spent every effort to avoid. 'Everything that I have worked for, everything that I have hoped for, everything that I have believed in during my public life, has crashed in ruins.'

It would have been better for himself and his reputation if he had immediately handed on the conduct of the war to another. (After all, Churchill was waiting in the wings.) He must have known that, such were the animosities which he had stirred in the Liberal and Labour forces, he could never lead a National Government. The last war should have taught him that no party Government could survive a long conflict. But such was his tenacity, or some would say obstinacy, that he clung to his position through the long months of the phoney war – September 1939 to May 1940 – and even after the first terrible outbreak of cataclysmic war with Hitler's invasion of Europe. Indeed he seems to have thought that the sudden change in the character of the war would enable him to retain power in spite of the weakening of his Parliamentary position.

I well remember those days, immediately following the critical division in the House of Commons, on 8 May, when the Government's majority, normally 200, fell to 81 with 33 of its supporters voting against. What would he do? We waited breathlessly. Brendan Bracken was a close friend of long standing, and I kept in touch with him. He was always contemptuous of Chamberlain whom he disliked; the 'Coroner' he used to call him, and indeed he seemed now to be likely to be enquiring into the cause of the death of a great nation. As the hours passed I would hear from time to time from Bracken how things were going. Chamberlain would not resign. It was like 'trying to get a limpet off a coffin sunk in the sea'. This, of course, was unfair. Yet even at the end I don't think Chamberlain understood the realities. The talk of Halifax as Prime Minister was absurd, not because he was a peer, but because he was absolutely unfitted to the task. To his credit he knew this, and resolutely refused to consider the idea. We needed the nearest thing to Marlborough, to Chatham, or Pitt, or Lloyd George. There he was ready to hand, marked out by destiny – Churchill.

CHAPTER SEVEN

Churchill

IF it is interesting to speculate what would have been the reputation in history of Baldwin and Neville Chamberlain had they retired a few years earlier, it is equally strange to reflect what would have been the standing of Churchill had his career ended before the outbreak of the Second World War. He would have been remembered as a man whose dazzling career just failed to reach the highest level. As brilliant as his father, Lord Randolph Churchill, and with more solid achievements to his credit, there would still necessarily have been drawn a comparison between the two men. The son's services to the Fleet in the opening years of the First War can never be forgotten; but his quarrel with Lord Fisher and the tragic failure of the Dardanelles stand on the other side of the account. Nor were they altogether compensated for by his work in the years of Lloyd George's Coalition, admirably as his talents were displayed over a wide area. Indeed many thought that Churchill was partly responsible for inciting or at least supporting his chief in the bold enterprise in Asia Minor which, it can be argued, almost brought about another war in the Chanak affair. After 1922, he seemed to go into the wilderness with Lloyd George's other friends and supporters; but he won his way back with his own inimitable courage. He came within an ace of winning a safe Conservative seat as an Independent, and finally was elected as a 'Constitutionalist' in the Election of 1924 which clothed his final return to the Conservative Party. Lloyd George used to say that a man 'cannot rat twice'. Churchill, who crossed the floor from the

Winston Churchill, 1923

Conservative to the Liberal Party in 1904, rejoined it in 1924. With the old Liberal Party in confusion and incipient decay, and his well-known antipathy to Socialism, Churchill's action was accepted as logical. But Lloyd George's generalisation was disproved in this particular instance. In any case, Churchill completed his political Odyssey over a decent period of time and with dignity. On a later occasion Sir William Jowitt was much criticised for a less elegant manoeuvre. Elected as a Liberal at a General Election, he took office the next day in a Labour Government. Churchill, sitting with some of his friends in the Smoking Room, took a more kindly view than they had expressed, but added: 'Poor fellow. He didn't know how to do it. Now if he had come to me, I could have instructed him in the technique of tergiversation.'

Five years later he was destined to dissociate himself from the official Conservative hierarchy over India. He strongly disapproved of the policies pursued by the Viceroy, and successive British Governments which, in his view, must lead to the severance of India from British rule and almost from any British connection. In this he stood almost alone with only a few 'diehard' friends to help him. Meanwhile, he had held high office as Chancellor of the Exchequer in Baldwin's Government of 1924 to 1929. There followed ten years, from 1929 to 1939, when he was out of office and out of favour. It must have seemed at this time that he could never return, and, after his loyal but ill-judged intervention in favour of King Edward VIII, when he was literally booed in the House of Commons, that his career was finished.

Then, at last, in 1940 there came to him that opportunity for which he seemed almost destined all his life. The world knows how he seized it and used it.

So much has been written about Churchill, including his own accounts of his active life in the six volumes of *The World Crisis* and the six volumes of *The Second World War*, in addition to the enchanting picture of his young days in *My Early Life*, that it seems unnecessary to add anything to this vast collection. Apart from the official life now in process of publication many writers have produced their own versions. The shelves of my library are

Speaking at a by-election, 1924

crowded with books about Churchill by all kinds of authors and in various languages. I shall therefore not attempt to do more than add some personal memories and try, however sketchily, to give some picture of him in these years of what seemed the end, but proved to be only the beginning, of his extraordinary career.

Although, as described, I had met a number of politicians and statesmen before entering the House in 1924 it so happened that I had never made any acquaintance with, and indeed had only once met, Churchill. He went to the Second Battalion of my regiment, the Grenadier Guards, under instruction before taking command of a battalion. This was after his exclusion from Lloyd George's War Government in 1916. I had already gone home wounded. But I soon heard that he made a deep impression on my fellow officers, and I was indeed unlucky not to be one to share this experience. I can recall the first time that I met Churchill in 1923. I can still remember the grace and courtesy with which he spoke to me about my uncle, Sir Frederick Macmillan, and the kindness which he had shown him over the publication in 1906 of his first important book, the life of Lord Randolph Churchill.

To everybody's astonishment, including his own, Churchill, in spite of his recent return to the fold, was appointed by Baldwin in 1924 to the great position now usually regarded as the second in the Government, of Chancellor of the Exchequer. He was said to have remarked that he had hoped for some kind of office but would have accepted the humble post of Chancellor of the Duchy. He was therefore in a buoyant mood. Baldwin had no doubt very good reasons for his choice. He had made his one great 'leap into the dark' in 1923, when he took a great risk for a great prize; but he had lost. In the Election of 1923 he had dissolved a Government which could have lasted for three years, in order to secure the public's approval for a protectionist policy which he declared was the only method by which unemployment could be cured. He never repeated this bold gesture. During the rest of his life, 'Safety First' became the slogan. Since in the 1924 Election the party had stood on a policy of so-called 'Safeguarding of Industry' and was honourably precluded from interpreting this principle so as to achieve a general tariff, Baldwin no doubt believed that he could best protect himself against the pressure of the strong protectionists, like Leo Amery, by securing the Treasury in the hands of a convinced free trader. With characteristic skill, even cunning, he

As Chancellor of the Exchequer with his family and Boothby

kept this balance throughout the whole Parliament. However, although full protection was precluded there were many opportunities for the exercise of the new Chancellor of the Exchequer's ingenuity. Meanwhile Churchill immediately began to make contacts with what was called the progressive group, the Young Conservatives whom he regarded as the natural inheritors of Tory democracy, his father's dream.

One of our members, Boothby, soon became his Parliamentary Private Secretary, and some of us began for the first time to enjoy, if not yet Churchill's friendship, at any rate the frequent opportunity for discussion in the most open and unconventional style in his company. While other Ministers seemed rather remote and stiff or conventional, anyone thrown into Churchill's presence felt immediately treated as an equal, encouraged to argue and debate like undergraduates amongst themselves, or with a young tutor; with no distinction of rank and without any inhibitions. For Churchill always regarded conversation as either an amusement, after a long day's work, or as an intellectual stimulus. Serious business was done by memorandum, by minute, by recorded decisions. He once said in the House of Commons during the Second War, 'I will be judged by my written words,' of which, indeed, the flow was enormous, sometimes embarrassing. But in these talks which I am recalling the most extravagant propositions could be put forward and repelled; the most novel ideas could be floated. It was half serious, half in fun. It was what lawyers would call 'without prejudice'. Yet, with his elephantine memory, Churchill never forgot anything that was said.

He had two remarkable private secretaries from the Treasury, Donald Ferguson and James Grigg, the latter destined to become Secretary of State for War in the great War Coalition. Both of these young men, especially the latter, treated the Chancellor of the Exchequer with little respect so far as argument was concerned, often proving him to be inaccurate, inconsistent and illogical. All the rest of us would sit round, sometimes late into the night, smoking, drinking and arguing, and of course listening. The flow of Churchill's rhetoric once it got under way was irresistible. Nevertheless, he quite happily allowed rival themes to be put forward in different parts of the room and took little notice of interruption. It was the first time that I had come across this kind of method of conducting political talk, and it was the beginning of a very long association which later ripened into close friendship with this man, the greatest figure and the greatest inspiration in my life.

In those days the battle raged chiefly on monetary policies. The pundits, especially from the Treasury and the Bank of England,

J. M. Keynes   *Sir Montagu Norman*

were determined to restore the Gold Standard and to bring sterling back to its old parity with the dollar. Under the influence of Keynes, who was an intimate friend of my brother Daniel and whom I too had known since a boy, I was led to doubt this policy. The most vehement and violent opponent against it among our group was Boothby, and among more experienced figures, Sir Robert Horne, a former Chancellor of the Exchequer. Mr Vincent Vickers, V.C., resigned from the Board of the Bank of England in protest. But there was little that we could do. It was my first Parliament, and I still had some of the modesty appropriate to young Members. The deflationary policy leading up to the re-establishment of a Gold Standard and the fixing of the value of the pound at 4.86 dollars was supported not only by the mass of the Conservative Party (who little understood the matter) but by Philip Snowden the former Labour Chancellor of the Exchequer who was the leading authority on the Labour side. It was my first experience of this sort. I have often since found that when a line of action is said to be supported 'by all responsible men' it is nearly always dangerous or foolish. So it was in this case; not merely because of the fixing of a rate which over-valued the pound, but because the preliminary steps to achieve this end involved years of steady deflation and increase in the value of sterling with all that this involved for the export industries. I think Churchill himself in his heart was uncertain. Indeed up to the end he hesitated. He was never unduly impressed by orthodox opinion. In the Budget debate, Alfred Mond, the ablest industrialist, was the only important critic on the Liberal side. Lloyd George later began to waver. Keynes's brilliant pamphlet *The Economic Consequences of Mr Churchill* was really an attack upon the man who dominated economic policy during this period, Montagu Norman, the Governor of the Bank. The fact is that being wholly ignorant of economics in its technical sense (the great period of economic experts and economic jargon was only just beginning), Churchill relied on instinctive feeling, mood and insight. Patriotism and pride made him give too much weight to the argument that we must 'make the pound look the dollar in the face'. But the more imaginative side of his nature made him susceptible to the objections which younger, and some more experienced, men were bringing against the whole policy. He also was, I think, a little suspicious that the policy was so heartily welcomed by Snowden, who was already showing himself in economic policy a Gladstonian Liberal rather than a Socialist. In his annoyance at Lloyd George's beginning to lean to the side of his critics, Churchill was goaded into a counter-attack in which he unwisely used these words: 'I never heard any argument more strange and so ill-founded, as that the Gold Standard is responsible for the condition of affairs in the coal industry. The Gold Standard is no more responsible than is the Gulf Stream.'

The dual weight of the Treasury and the Bank of England were too much for the Chancellor of the Exchequer at that time. Then these authorities were regarded as enjoying almost divine inspiration. The famous Governor of the Bank, who contrary to all the old traditions of the Bank of England was re-elected year after year had become a sort of dictator. The orthodox Treasury view, free trade, accompanied by deflationary finance, was really based upon nineteenth-century principles. What could two or three leading figures of the older generation or a few young men do on

The coalminers' strike

the other side, even if backed by Keynes, who was himself suspect among many of the older economists?

Of course I would only have watched this from the outside had it not been for the intimacy which Churchill allowed some of the younger ones amongst us. It was my first experience of a great political issue being fought out by all the different methods which are brought to bear on a question, and it was truly fascinating. Alas, the critics were right, and there followed almost inevitably the coal dispute and the General Strike.

The actual handling of the General Strike was one of the memorable achievements of Baldwin. With his sympathy, his understanding and his steadiness he saved a strike from drifting into a revolt. In this grave issue Churchill did not show the same calm appreciation of the underlying realities. When the newspapers were stopped, there was launched the *British Gazette* which was under his control; many people thought it a somewhat violent if effective organ. The truth is that the General Strike was a battle; and Churchill's idea of a battle was something on which you should not hesitate but win as soon as possible. He believed that a show of force could intimidate the strikers; while Baldwin felt, and more correctly, that the leaders of most of the trade unions were only too anxious to find an excuse for peace. There was a dispute in the Cabinet as to encouraging the Territorial Army to serve as a reserve to the police. They were to wear ordinary clothes with armbands. Churchill was put in charge of the sub-committee to make the arrangements and a plan was soon devised; but the collapse of the strike made it unnecessary. There was much attack later upon the tone and temper of the *British Gazette*. It was certainly a useful, indeed the only instrument for disseminating Government policy, since the radio was not yet in any general use. How well I remember the small cats' whiskers and black boxes, and the continual crackling noises, with which we tried to listen to Savoy Hill. Churchill defended his journal with a characteristic remark in a later debate when the crisis was over. 'I decline utterly to be impartial between the fire brigade and the fire,' and then with that inimitable touch of almost schoolboy cheekiness he went on to say, 'I have no wish to make threats or to use language which would disturb the House or cause bad blood, but this I must say: Make your minds perfectly clear that if ever you let loose upon us again a general strike, we will loose upon you – another *British Gazette*.'

If Churchill took a somewhat sterner attitude than Baldwin and others of his colleagues during the crisis it was due partly to his temperament and partly to a less accurate appreciation than Baldwin's of the real feelings of the trade union leaders. In effect their hearts were not in the fight, and Baldwin knew it. Yet, when

The British Gazette

Published by His Majesty's Stationery Office.

LONDON, WEDNESDAY, MAY 12, 1926.   ONE PENNY.

ORDER AND QUIET THROUGH THE LAND.

Growing Dissatisfaction Among The Strikers.

INCREASING NUMBERS OF MEN RETURNING TO WORK.

850 Omnibuses In The Streets Of London.

MORE AND MORE TRAINS.

OFFICIAL COMMUNIQUE.

WHITEHALL, May 11.

The situation throughout the country shows a further improvement. The distribution of food supplies gives no cause whatever for apprehension. There have been a few reports of temporary local shortages of particular commodities, but on investigation it has been found that the majority of these reports are inaccurate, and in the remaining cases the necessary steps have been at once taken to make the position secure. Especially large supplies of sugar were distributed yesterday.

The situation at the ports is entirely satisfactory, and there is a growing confidence among traders as to their ability to move goods confided to them without the direct assistance of the Government.

The distribution of petrol is proceeding more rapidly than at any previous period of the General Strike.

There has been no interruption of the power services, and traffic on railways is continuously increasing. Apart from the unrelieved...

WORK AS USUAL.

Tour Through Agricultural England.

FOOD FOR THE TOWNS.

(By a "British Gazette" Representative.)

A dash by road through the Eastern Counties of England brings home something of the magnitude of the task which has to be faced in feeding London. All through the day the rumble of great lorries is heard in this powerful agricultural area, including the Counties of Norfolk, Suffolk, Cambridgeshire, Huntingdonshire and Essex, to feed the millions in the cities. In the evening the stream is reversed and this time the empty vehicles are radiating steadily from London to pick up more of their precious freight, and so it goes on.

In a run from London, via Cambridge and Ely to Hunstanton, I did not see a single breakdown or lorry held up for an accident, and considering the volume of traffic this is a remarkable achievement on the part of the drivers. It was a testimony to the remarkably high standard of driving. The lorries were, without exception, handled with great skill, and their drivers were always courteous in making way for faster traffic, so that the overtaking of a group of a dozen or more of these heavy vehicles held no terrors for the drivers of lighter and faster cars.

BUSY MARKET TOWNS.

The agricultural people of the district were carrying on their work in a normal manner, and everywhere I heard the opinion expressed that the trouble would soon be over. In Norfolk great droves of cattle were being driven along the roads to the...

TO-DAY'S CARTOON.

By BERNARD PARTRIDGE

UNDER WHICH FLAG?

JOHN BULL. ONE OF THESE TWO FLAGS HAS GOT TO COME DOWN—AND IT WON'T BE MINE.

(By Courtesy of the Proprietors of "Punch.")

LEGAL ISSUE OF THE STRIKE.

Sir H. Slesser against Discussion.

THE TRADE DISPUTES ACT.

WESTMINSTER, Monday.

On the motion for the adjournment of the House of Commons, the legal aspect of the General Strike was raised.

Sir H. Slesser referred in the speech made by Sir J. Simon, on Thursday evening last, on the subject of the law as it applied to trade disputes. He said that the legislature had decided that when a trade dispute existed, the procurement of a breach of contract was not in itself an illegal matter. Whether this act was lawful or unlawful must depend on whether the trade dispute came within the definition of the Trade Disputes Act.

That was a matter to be decided by a court of law. Under the existing law, in the case of every trade union, no member could recover benefits as present.

He thought that it was most unfortunate that the legal question had been introduced at all at this juncture. He desired that the settlement, which he hoped would now be achieved in this matter, should not be prejudiced by anything that might adversely be decided by a court of law.

Sir Gordon Cosens suggested that Sir H. Slesser had not given notice to the Attorney-General that he intended to raise this matter so that he could be present.

A SIGNAL CONTRIBUTION.

Sir Douglas Hogg (the Attorney-General), who said he had only been given two minutes notice that the matter was to be raised, did not claim that it was unfortunate Sir J. Simon should have made the speech he did. His view was that the John's speech was a signal contribution to the knowledge of the public as to the true facts surrounding the present dispute, and that he did a great public service in stating in clear and unequivocal language what is his view was the law as he saw it.

It would not be right, however, for Sir Douglas, holding the post he did, to say just what he believed to be the law in regard to the present position. It was his responsibility to advise the Government...

AMONG THE MINERS.

Uneventful Days in Yorkshire.

MEN ANXIOUS TO RETURN.

No Trouble Expected.

(By a "British Gazette" Special Representative.)

I have just returned to London after a week spent in Barnsley—the centre of the mining industry in the West Riding of Yorkshire and the headquarters of the Yorkshire Miners' Association.

I left London hastily by the first train after the declaration of the strike on May 1, anticipating trouble in this district; but it has been entirely uneventful—a week spent in the midst of people who are newly distressed at the upheaval, but are anxious to preserve order and to return, as soon as possible, to normal working conditions.

The train by which I travelled north was well filled with people who were leaving for their homes at the first hint of trouble; but there was no panic. Barnsley was spending a quiet week-end; it took the inhabitants some days to realise that a strike had been proclaimed, and they wandered happily enough about the town, filling the picture theatres, and looking for the football results more eagerly than for the strike news.

At first there was a certain air of excitement throughout the town. The men were beginning to realise that there was little hope of a general...

it was all over and the coal strike dragged on month after month, Baldwin with his usual relapse after a great crisis made little effort to find a solution. I remember well in the summer of that year Churchill's determination to make a new effort to find a settlement. In August, when Baldwin was safely at Aix-les-Bains, he was left in charge. He grasped eagerly at the chance of solving the dispute. There seemed at one moment to be every hope of achieving this. In September he urged strongly on Baldwin that some action must be taken; but with his colleagues hesitant and standing almost unsupported except for a few of his friends on the backbenches he was unsuccessful. The dispute dragged on to its melancholy end when the men gradually began to drift back to work, district by district.

Other parts of his work as Chancellor of the Exchequer were more successful. His Budgets while avoiding the forbidden ground of Protection showed great ingenuity and elasticity of mind. His Budget speeches were marvels of carefully devised argument and sometimes splendid rhetoric. Although some of his devices were thought by many to be almost too clever, yet the great schemes for widows' and orphans' pensions were well received by Parliament and the country. At this time his standing in the Conservative Party, considering the animosities of the past, was remarkably high. His wit, his artistry and his vigorous personality intrigued and fascinated Members of all parties, especially the new Members, who had never known him in war or pre-war days. Yet there was still some suspicion, especially among the old Conservative Members, and among the more rabid of the Socialists. There was an element of puritanism at that time in the trade union movement based upon the chapel. They somehow suspected any man who could deal with great affairs in so dextrous and even flamboyant a manner.

My next contact with Churchill was over the 'De-rating of Industry' scheme. Some proposals of mine in casual conversation had given him the idea, as he was generous enough to declare. I had argued in one of our talks that the existing system of rating fell too heavily upon productive industry, especially since much of the cost of looking after the unemployed and the poor fell upon the local rates. The attraction to Churchill was to find a method of helping the heavy industries without Protection. He took me into his confidence from the start, and I was able to follow the development of the scheme with all its complexities. Naturally there were sometimes conflicts between him and Neville Chamberlain, then Minister of Health. Chamberlain was more interested in the reform of local government than in the question of the burden of rates upon industry. I had argued my point in small meetings with the Chancellor of the Exchequer and had pressed it into speeches and articles for more than two years. When Churchill began to revolve this in his mind he pressed forward vigorously with his plan. By the end of 1927 almost all of the Cabinet except Balfour and Birkenhead were against him, and he was in rather a despondent mood. He did not wish to run his head against an impassable barrier. Baldwin remembered the General Election of 1923; Churchill also remembered the Gallipoli campaign when he 'found himself all alone when the wind of criticism began to blow'.

On 11 December 1927 I sent him a memorandum setting out my views. I had only now been three years in Parliament and I can still recall the thrill of pleasure of receiving on 5 January 1928 the following reply:

It is always pleasant to find someone whose mind grasps the essentials and proportions of a large plan. I made you party to it because I was sure you would enrich its preliminary discussion, and also because – though you may have forgotten it – a chance remark of yours about the rating system, made more than two years ago, first implanted in my mind the seed of what may become a considerable event.

Broadly speaking we are agreed on the lines advocated in your 'Finance of the Scheme'. In fact your statement under this head tallies almost identically with the decisions and arguments which quite separately I have arrived at here . . .

He went on to say:

If you will call at the Treasury when next you are in London, my private office will show you all my papers on this subject and you can read them there . . . I am now planning to bring this matter before the Cabinet on the 11th or 12th, and to ask for a Committee of five or six to study it with me . . .

I followed up my previous letter on 2 January 1928 with a further memorandum in support of Churchill's proposals as to the form which the industrial contribution should take. He replied on 15 January as follows:

I considered your statement of the pros and cons for the Profits Tax versus leaving one-third on the Rates so lucid and well balanced that I sent it to the Prime Minister. I thought it would interest you to know that he spoke to me about it on Thursday in extremely complimentary terms . . .

It was this power to use and encourage young men as well as to put aside any question of his dignity when large matters were under discussion that was for me one of Churchill's greatest attractions. The De-rating Scheme went through in due course after several clashes with Neville Chamberlain on one of which I was sufficiently involved to earn a somewhat severe reproof from the Minister. Even then I could not help comparing the two men. To sit and talk to Churchill was like young men at Oxford arguing with dons or even professors – and plenty of drink and cigars provided. To be sent for to Neville Chamberlain's room was more like an interview with the headmaster.

As the Parliament was reaching its end, in spite of its successful work I felt strongly, even in my inexperience, that we could not hope to hold the industrial cities in the Midlands and the north of England without a more forward policy than that which seemed likely to be proposed by Baldwin and the party organisation. It was true that in these five years there had been some great reforms – poor law, rating, the pension scheme and the rest. There had also been in the public mind some sad episodes. The long-drawn-out coal dispute, the continued troubles of the exporting industries and the heavy burden of unemployment. If the party managers thought they could win the cities north of the Trent on the policy of 'Safety First', they were much mistaken. Therefore it seemed to me that everything would turn on the Budget of April 1929.

I remember well a visit to Chartwell where he had kindly invited me to come to lunch and explain my ideas. J. L. Garvin, the famous editor of the *Observer*, was there and one or two others; but no officials. After luncheon, he allowed me to expound my case. Nor did he interrupt my exposition or allow any of the other guests to do so. I put forward in the best Keynesian terms I could the arguments for reflation and expansion, even, at some risk, to accept any resulting pressure on sterling; the mere fact of so much capacity of men and machinery being unused gave us an opportunity for an expansionist policy without the dangers of inflation. All this I argued to the best of my ability, without any attempt at either wit or brilliance. He listened thoughtfully, and turned to Garvin who strongly supported my appeal. I ended by saying that if his April Budget, the last Budget of the Parliament, proved not to be a merely humdrum Budget but showed a touch of imagination and some real hope for the poor depressed areas of Britain, we had a chance of a successful Election and the beginning of an industrial and commercial recovery. If we took the lead, perhaps other countries would follow. Then Garvin argued on the same lines volubly and effectively. Churchill still said nothing. Finally he said, 'Well, I think I know what you mean. After all the national affairs are like the affairs of the family. There are the great spending departments in each; and at the end of each year father and mother sit down to compare the expenses with the family income. Sometimes this leads to bitter disputes. "Why so much spent on the children's dresses or on their amusement?" "Well," the wife replies, "Why so much on brandy and cigars?" The husband indignantly asserts that brandy and cigars are the staff of life, the defence of the home like the Army, Navy and Air Force. So the dispute goes on, each side denouncing the other side's expenditure. Finally there is silence; a serious rift in a hitherto happy and united family seems unavoidable. Then with one united gesture, father, mother and children fling up their hands and cry "My God, let's go and borrow from the bank."' 'That,' he said, 'I understand to be the general tenor of your argument.' We agreed; and so in his heart did he, but there was no result. The Budget of April 1929 abolished the tax on tea, but nobody was in the least grateful. What my people in Stockton and in the depressed areas wanted was not a penny or two off tea, but work and wages instead of the perpetual dole.

There followed in Churchill's life ten years from May 1929 to September 1939, when he held no public office, although for eight years of this time the Conservative Party with its allies was in power.

During the first part of that period I saw him from time to time, and being a near neighbour of his often went over to Chartwell. But I could not support the attitude he took about the future of India. It seemed to me however desirable, to be impracticable, and that the whole of British policy was logically involved in the concept of self-government as an ultimate end in the Dominions and Colonies alike. How slow would be the progress or how rapid was a matter for argument. The argument was in fact settled by the Second World War. In any case during these years I was myself involved almost entirely on the struggle for economic reconstruction and recovery. When I spoke in the debate in March 1933 demanding a more expansionist policy Churchill took the trouble to come down and give me some support; but his mind was moving rapidly from economic and financial to political problems. Soon after his fight over India there came the rise of the Nazi Party. It started as a small cloud and was soon to develop into a menacing and fearful storm.

This remarkable man with unbounded energy during these years not only completed the four long volumes of his life of Marlborough, in itself a heavy task (they were published from 1933 to 1938), but also organised almost single-handed a campaign in opposition to the Government's Indian policy. However, with the passage of the India Act, which in any case was not to take effect for some years, it might have been thought, to use Churchill's own words, that 'the barrier' between him and the majority of his Conservative colleagues 'had fallen away'. From this time, till the Second World War, I saw him with increasing frequency and intimacy.

As the Election of 1935 approached there was much talk in Conservative circles, officially and unofficially, about Churchill's future. Did they want him to assist in the rearmament which was now clearly necessary, or were they more frightened of him than they were of Hitler and Mussolini? It would be perhaps too cynical to declare that Baldwin's decision would largely depend upon the size of the Conservative majority. If it was sufficiently large, they would do without him. If it were narrow, they would find him a useful ally. Nevertheless Churchill's isolation during these years had already produced tragic results. His reliance upon the extreme Right of his party on the Indian issue injured his position with the party as a whole, as well as with Liberal and non-party feeling in the country. Although he had now turned to the new German threat and the need for rapid rearmament, yet he was still, especially to many unimaginative minds, an object of suspicion. It was easy

Churchill at leisure : bricklaying

for the Establishment, the mediocrities who surrounded Baldwin, to harp upon Churchill's alleged impetuosity and lack of judgment. Geoffrey Dawson, one of Baldwin's chief cronies, shared this view, and as Editor of *The Times* made it public. 'Winston would be a disruptive force, especially since foreign relations and defence would be uppermost.' The seeds of appeasement were already being sown.

Then Churchill began a campaign in the House of Commons on foreign policy which no one who heard it would ever forget. When he turned to rearmament, he carried on almost alone a struggle of outstanding vigour and resilience. Moreover the House, whether they approved or not of his views, could not but be amazed at the width and accuracy of his knowledge. But he made little progress. I used always to come in to hear these speeches, but since I was concentrating on my own work of internal reconstruction and reform I made no attempt to take part in these debates. The Conservative back-benchers were sympathetic and in their heart agreed with Churchill. The front bench put on that look of shocked disapproval which so often makes Ministers in such a period look like somewhat supercilious camels. The official Labour and Liberal view was of course unsympathetic. The ruling doctrine was that we should rely for our defence against any aggressor upon 'collective security' to be organised by the League of Nations. But it did not seem to occur to Ministers that our contributions to this combined effort must be based upon reality. If Germany and Italy were to prove the aggressors, if Russia's position were to remain enigmatic, where would the security come from? Attlee who was very fond of using this phrase never explained this vital point. He seemed to think that being a little remote from Europe we should at any rate pay a smaller subscription being, as it were, 'country members' of the club.

These great philippics on defence and foreign policy can still be studied with advantage, not only for their content but also for their style. Many of my friends and I were moved by the sight of this man fighting alone, and did our best to give him at any rate the support of our presence in the House, where amongst the large number of well-meaning men of ability and some distinction there were only two great giants. There were respectable hills and mountains, but only two oustanding peaks – Lloyd George and Churchill. It seems strange that for these vital years neither should be able to exert any effective influence upon any official party in the House of Commons.

Nevertheless it must be admitted that the Western Allies still contained a considerable superiority of power. Indeed there was no doubt until after 1936, that fatal period of hesitation which enabled Hitler to remilitarise the Rhineland and thus block any effective action in support of their Eastern Allies by the French armies, that Hitler's aggression could still be effectively checked, if at some risk. During this tangled period Churchill had not an easy role to play; but as the situation gradually darkened more and more Members of Parliament on both sides of the House began to look eagerly for his advice. Since my activities with The Next Five Years Group led me to meet many people of the Right, Centre and Left, I was able to judge a growing sense of alarm. The most unlikely people who had been contented with vague platitudes began to look more and more for guidance from this stormy petrel.

On the question of Abyssinia and the abandonment of that country to the Italian invader, Churchill was torn like many other realists between the importance of supporting the policy upon which we had embarked and the hope even at this late hour of keeping Italy and Germany apart. Certainly Britain's policy had been strangely feeble. After all the talk of stopping the dictators, the League had entirely failed.

The most vivid recollection that I have of Churchill at this time apart from his continual willingness to discuss with me my own affairs – I was hard at work on my book *The Middle Way* – was his tremendous application and the admirable system which he had devised for obtaining as a private citizen information not always available even to a Minister.

On 7 April 1939, a week after Chamberlain, finding his policy of appeasement in ruins, gave the famous guarantee to Poland,

Mussolini invaded Albania. I was lunching with Churchill at Chartwell when the news came of the Italian landings. It was a scene that gave me my first picture of Churchill at work. Maps were brought out; secretaries were marshalled; telephones began to ring. 'Where was the British fleet?' That was the most urgent question. That considerable staff which, even as a private individual, Churchill always maintained to support his tremendous outflow of literary and political effort was at once brought into play. It turned out that the British fleet was scattered throughout the Mediterranean. Of the five great ships, one was at Gibraltar, one in the Eastern Mediterranean, and the remaining three, in Churchill's words, 'lolling about inside or outside widely-separated Italian ports'. A few days later he criticised these dispositions in a powerful speech in the House of Commons.

I shall always have a picture of that spring day and the sense of power and energy, the great flow of action, which came from Churchill, although he then held no public office. He alone seemed to be in command, when everyone else was dazed and hesitating. Lord Halifax's first reaction to Mussolini's blow was as characteristic as Churchill's. He is said to have exclaimed, when he heard of the sudden and treacherous attack: 'And on Good Friday too!' The British Ambassador was instructed to deliver a memorandum of which Ciano wrote in his diary that it 'might have been composed in our own offices'. Italian policy was generally based on bluff and should certainly have been dealt with by determined action. As Bismarck – rather brutally – said of Italians, 'They have a big appetite and poor teeth'. It was certainly true of Mussolini.

But it remains true that the fatal date was the military occupation of the Rhineland. Up to that time and perhaps a year or two later, when the defences would be completed, it was still possible for the French Army to impose its will. We know the terror of the German generals at the time. They could not believe that the Western world would fail to see the vast strategic importance of a fortified Rhineland. All the other breaches of faith or acts of aggression of Hitler up to this date were of minor importance. This gave him the occupation of the vital position and immensely

The reoccupation of the Rhineland

weakened the power of the Western Allies to intervene in any issue
in the future. Strangely enough our Government did not seem to
understand this. Even Lloyd George did not grasp it fully. With
different men at the top a bold decision would have been taken at
this vital date – March 1936. Had Churchill and Barthou been in

power in London and Paris strong action would undoubtedly have been taken and the Second World War and all that has flowed from it might have been avoided. If Hitler's bluff had been called, nothing could have prevented his fall. But alas, after all their deliberations, after the mountains had been in labour, only a little mouse was born. Meetings of French and British Ministers; talks between French and British staffs; a protest to the League of Nations at the breach of the Locarno Treaty – that was all. On the vital question of rearmament, instead of Churchill's recall, which almost all of us expected, Sir Thomas Inskip was appointed, in hopeless conditions, to a supreme task. The situation was well summed up in a quotation from Neville Chamberlain's diary.

The events of the weekend [occupation of the Rhineland by Hitler] afforded an excellent reason for discarding both Winston and Sam since both had European reputations which might make it dangerous to add them to the Cabinet at a critical moment. Inskip would create no jealousies. He would excite no enthusiasm but he would involve us in no fresh perplexities.

It must have been a bitter reflection for Churchill all through the terrible years that followed to consider the wasted opportunities and their tragic results. When he called the Second World War 'the unnecessary war' it was not a phrase thrown off in a moment of exasperation. It was the result of long and careful deliberation after a full review of the whole tragic story.

These then are my memories of Churchill from his return to the Conservative Government in 1924, through his five years at the Treasury, through the ten years of isolation devoted to a combination of immense historical composition and a magnificent series of speeches based on careful research, up to the outbreak of war.

Where, one might reflect, would Churchill have stood in history had he been successful in pressing his views on his old colleagues, Baldwin and Chamberlain. Had France and Britain nerved themselves while resistance was still easy, had the war been avoided, the world taken a new turn, what could have been Churchill's role? It is difficult now to judge. Certainly if he had died in 1938 he would have gone down to history as a brilliant politician with much achievement to his credit, although many failures also to account for. He would have been remembered as an orator, writer, historian and as a Minister who had played a part in great events. But so strange are the vagaries of life that the supreme position that he holds in the history of Britain and Europe has been based upon the utter failure of the policies which he pressed upon his fellow countrymen in these decisive years. If sometimes 'nothing succeeds like success', at other times it would appear that 'nothing succeeds like failure'.

CHAPTER EIGHT

Parliament and Power

I HAVE already described some of the features of electioneering fifty years ago, and the different conditions in which General Elections were held. Each constituency, especially in the provinces, was largely self-contained; it held its own series of meetings indoors and outdoors, without much contact with the rest of the country or even the neighbouring areas. I remember very well, once an election had started, feeling as if a great shutter had come down between us and the rest of the world. There we were, isolated in Stockton, working away day after day, night after night, in what seemed a sort of fog. (One had something of the same experience in a great battle, like Loos or the Somme.) Naturally pamphlets and propaganda papers were sent to us from Central Office (if we paid for them, which we were loath to do) but very few were much good to us. It was better to print short and simple messages attuned to our own needs. Even Middlesbrough and Sedgefield seemed far away. Little news came through as to how the campaign was going over the rest of the country. In each constituency separate engagements were being waged without much regard for the main armies.

Generally, we held three or four meetings a night in small schoolrooms, ill-adapted to the purpose, always full, usually rowdy and making quite a considerable strain upon the nervous system of a tyro. For some reason the school official, either because he was a Socialist or from a perverted sense of humour, generally only made available the infants' school, where the seating was

ELECTIONEERING UP-TO-DATE.

Capt. Harold Macmillan, the Conservative candidate for Stockton, addressing a street corner audience in Ewbank-street, through a microphone and loud speaker.

ill-suited to the ample forms of the audience. In addition to a few afternoon meetings and some women's meetings, there was the perpetual canvassing, through one street after another. It was thought a great novelty to use a loudspeaker, which was done by fixing a trumpet to the front of the car and standing at the back speaking through a microphone. Incidentally this mechanism was continually going wrong and could easily be interfered with by malevolent (especially juvenile) critics.

In the counties an almost equally arduous campaign involved visiting five or six villages a night. Here the technique was that the supporting speakers should keep the meeting going until the arrival of the candidate, who would spend perhaps twenty or twenty-five minutes at each place and then rush off hopefully to the next, trusting there would be no breakdown in the car.

Of course, occasionally we had an outside speaker at a big rally but naturally the supply of distinguished speakers was quite inadequate to the demand and most of us had to battle on alone. Moreover, outside speakers must be carefully chosen. They could easily do more harm than good.

As regards the Press, in Teesside the local newspapers were far more important than the national. Some more prosperous

May I appeal to **YOU** to VOTE for my Husband.

I know that he will serve **YOU** faithfully and carry out all he has promised to do.

DOROTHY MACMILLAN.

Printed & Published by Ed. Appleby, Prince Regent St., Stockton. 7673-23

'*Short and simple messages attuned to our own needs*'

families might 'take in' the *Daily Mail*, or even the *Daily Telegraph*; but the mass of the people scarcely bothered with a morning paper, unless perhaps a picture paper. From the political point of view the important journal was the *North Eastern Daily Gazette*, an evening paper which gave the vital football and racing news

Listening to election results, 1931

of universal interest. But at Election time they would print reports of the progress of the contests in neighbouring constituencies.

In the early years the radio had hardly begun to make an impact. Some people had equipped themselves with a little black box, like a Brownie camera, with what were called 'cats whiskers' which imperfectly received and distributed the news and parts of speeches or separate addresses from the party leaders. I don't think it had much influence, and few of the leading politicians had yet learned to use this medium properly. The only one who did so was Baldwin. Most of them seemed to think they were making speeches to millions of people. Baldwin was the first to realise that the audience for a radio or later television broadcast is seldom more than two or three. There might be father, mother and perhaps a daughter, or perhaps only husband and wife, sitting in a room. That is the true audience. Even if it is multiplied five or six million times, one is still talking to a few individuals in a room, not orating to a mass gathered in a hall.

Sometimes in the last week of the campaign some press revelation or stunt could be important. For instance the *Daily Mail*'s threat to disclose the Zinoviev letter forced the Foreign Office to publish it immediately.

In a way, elections up to the Second War were much more like elections throughout the eighteenth and nineteenth centuries. They were jolly, rowdy, and exciting. The party system was strong but not as strong as it became later. Individual candidates counted for more. Well known or even eccentric people like Lord Henry Bentinck could carry what seemed a clearly Labour constituency because of the deep affection which he inspired. Even I was able to hold Stockton in 1935 on a non-party programme compiled by a group of friends, and bring to my platform Conservatives, Liberals and even the old Independent Labour Party intellectual, Lord Allen of Hurtwood. This larger degree of independence is accounted for partly by the genuine sense of local pride and local interest before it had been squeezed out by the hydra of local government reform, with units too extended to preserve any reality.

Moreover in those days the different parties, while each maintained a central fund, financed the local election expenses in different ways. In the Labour Party most of the expenditure fell upon party funds, largely subscribed by the trade unions' political contributions. Many, if not the majority, of the candidates were 'sponsored' by a particular trade union. In the Conservative and Liberal Parties, either funds were raised locally assisted by some contributions from headquarters, or the candidates were themselves responsible for part or all the election expenses. Expenses were comparatively small, and money was still valuable. Some of the Conservative Members were rich; others men of modest fortunes. But nearly all had some income of their own. But £2,000

Campaigning in Stockton, 1935

a year, now hardly a labourer's wage, would have been a substantial income for the younger son of good family. Moreover since the payment of Members was only £300, later raised to £400 a year, this was not in itself sufficient to attract professionals. We were all more or less amateurs brought into Parliamentary life by a number of motives; but the making of a satisfactory financial career was certainly not one of them.

The great Press Lords, Rothermere and Beaverbrook, had considerable power, mostly south of the Trent and generally rated above its true value. They certainly alarmed the party machines and some of the party leaders. Undoubtedly their large circulations gave them the opportunity to bully even, some might say, blackmail the unhappy politicians. But the more sober Berrys, with the *Daily Telegraph* and the *Sunday Times*, were less unpredictable. *The Times* depended on the editor, after it passed from Northcliffe to John Astor, not on the proprietor.

Churchill always cultivated the Press and had good relations with the Press magnates, partly because he had a high opinion of their influence and partly because he depended upon them in certain periods of his life for a substantial part of his income. He was always romantically attracted by the bizarre character of some of these personalities. Baldwin hated the Press and had a contempt for it, with the exception, of course, of *The Times* and his close friend Geoffrey Dawson, his *fidus Achates*. The radio in itself had little power. In the hands of a skilful operator like Baldwin it could be almost decisive; but that was a radio wielded as an instrument by one of the contenders. It had not in itself great influence, and under Sir John Reith's austere control it was managed with scrupulous fairness. Television at this period had not yet begun to exert its strange fascination.

There survived certainly up to the Second World War something of the old political life that had dominated English politics for two centuries or more. The leading figures of the great parties were like Homeric heroes fighting in single combat with each other, leading their armies to attack, encouraging them in retreat and rallying them to counter-attack. Much also remained of the personal rivalries. Gladstone and Disraeli, Gladstone and Salisbury, and similar contests had dominated the end of the nineteenth century. Later the leading figures, Lloyd George, Churchill, MacDonald and Baldwin did not fall short from these older leaders in the interest they evoked in the public mind. Today, with few exceptions, they seem somewhat shadowy and transient phantoms.

Where then did power lie? The Church of England had lost

Churchill and Northcliffe

both its political unity and its political importance. The old convention of squire and parson was fading in the countryside, and non-existent in the towns. If the older clergy were probably inclined to conservatism, the younger were attracted to radicalism and even dabbled in more advanced doctrines.

In the Midlands and in the North the chapel was still powerful. Lloyd George tried to found his final bid for power in 1935 upon the Free Churches as a nucleus. In certain constituencies, especially where the great parties were nicely balanced, Roman Catholic minorities could often exert great influence, being sometimes strong enough to settle the issue. On the economic side forces of industry and commerce were, of course, still important, although not yet highly organised. The tariff controversy had made a bitter division from the moment when it was launched by Joseph Chamberlain in 1902 up to the final settlement by the National Government in 1931. Broadly speaking the exporting industries inclined to Free Trade, while the home industries naturally clamoured for Protection.

Finally, the trade unions. Although the Act of the Liberal Government of 1906, reversing the Taff Vale decision and putting unions and, more important, union funds, more or less outside the law, had given a great impetus to their power. Yet their strength was rarely abused. The great national disputes of 1910 and 1911 had been alarming but were settled partly by the skill of Lloyd George and partly by the inherent moderation of the union leaders. They were, after all, still fighting in many cases for recognition; that is to establish themselves as the negotiating party on behalf of the workers. The same remained true up till the General Strike. After its failure, the authority of the moderate leaders was further enhanced.

In the First War the trade unions used their power moderately. Although the wages of munition workers increased dramatically, yet the fact that many millions of men were serving in the forces at almost nominal pay and were mostly volunteers, had its effect on the morale of those at home. Some of the more transient recruits to industrial life, the women munition workers and the like, were

THE
ROBERT
BROWNING SETTLEMENT

WALWORTH

STANDS FOR THE
LABOUR MOVEMENT
IN RELIGION.

'*More advanced doctrines*'

said to have earned extravagant sums, but after all this was but an ephemeral symptom.

After the collapse of the post-war boom in 1923 until the beginnings of significant rearmament in 1937 economic conditions did not favour any attempt by the trade unions to exploit their industrial, still less to seize political, power. It is often forgotten, indeed it seems hardly credible to the younger generation, that the great struggles between the wars were not about the increase of wages but to determine the measure of their decrease. The deflationary policy recommended by the Bank of England and accepted by the Treasury and Parliament led to a long period of stable or falling prices. This consideration, together with world-wide depression, put so heavy a handicap on exports that the unions were more anxious to keep employment going than to fight for wage rises that could only bring ruin both to the employers and the employed.

The coal strike of 1926, which led to the General Strike, resulted from the employers' demand for either longer hours or reduction of wages, or both, in order to be able to preserve the export markets (for it should not be forgotten that a great part of the coal raised was normally sold abroad). The French occupation of the Ruhr had given a short but artificial boom to coal exports. When the French abandoned this exercise the slump returned. Moreover the structure of industry, especially public utilities, made it much more difficult for extreme or subversive union leaders to threaten complete disruption by strike action. Certainly the railways could be partially paralysed; but they could usually organise some kind of service by voluntary action, aiding the officials who stayed at work. For instance, during one railway strike, the Underground was operated by volunteers. The docks could be a serious threat; but they too could be kept open by troops. As regards power, gas or electric, there was no grid or national distribution. It was quite easy to operate a local plant with a few men taken either from the management or from the services. As regards industry there had not yet been organised the incredibly complicated system by which, for instance, motor car production is carried on. For

Trade union rally, 1933

assembly plants relying on their daily supply of parts of all kinds and descriptions, the interference of one of which will bring the whole mechanism to a stop, the situation is precarious and an easy target for extremist or 'unofficial' strikers. Between the wars, partly as a result of the long depression, stocks were high in most industries. When the great coal strike of 1926 began there was a year's supply of coal above ground.

All these circumstances depressed or at any rate did not tend to increase the power of militant trade unionism. Moreover the General Strike of 1926, although it only lasted a week, gave the whole nation a shock. The trade union leaders were determined never to repeat it.

All this has been changed by a number of factors in addition to the technical changes in production methods. First, full employment has automatically increased the power of the unions. Secondly, a period when prices have either risen slowly but steadily, or later with dramatic rapidity, combined with the loss of value or even confidence in money, has altered the position. Thirdly, the tactical and even strategic strength of certain classes of workmen such as the gas and electric light workers, as well as the miners, and even the sewer workers or the transport workers, can bring about something like a standstill and hold the whole nation to ransom. Fourthly, the great swing to the Left in schools, colleges, universities, the Press and literature has in recent years been accompanied in the trade unions by the capture of some and the threat to others by Communist forces. In this situation Parliament, which was supreme in the years with which I am concerned, is itself threatened. What the politicians decide cannot necessarily be enforced. The trade unions who have in their hands the key to survival can prove more powerful than the Ministers who affect the outward trappings of authority, without in fact being able to exercise decisive influence on events. Within the last few years a great trade union, the miners, had defeated a Conservative Government once and a Labour Government twice. The electorate as a whole seems to accept the situation, without violent protest or reaction.

This leads naturally to the question where does power now reside, or, to use the language of the older writers, where does 'sovereignty' lie? The true answer no doubt is that it has never resided in any one particular group. Always throughout our history it has been a struggle; but it would not perhaps be extravagant to say that the conflict has been between those acting or claiming to act on behalf of the nation as a whole against internal groups, of whatever character, organised to pursue their own vested interests. For instance, the long struggle of the Middle Ages between the Crown and the Church was not a matter of doctrine; it was a matter of practical administration. The Church claimed exemption from taxation; it claimed its own courts in which all men who were 'clerks' (that is broadly literate) however low the degree of their order, could demand the right of trial, instead of the King's courts. The battle lasted for centuries, with gains and losses on either side. Similarly, the King controlling Westminster, London and the Home Counties, found even in Tudor times that his writ did not really run to the distant areas. The great barons and nobles of the north or of the west, the Percys and the like, could almost defy him. This contest for power lasted long, but in the end the central authority proved victorious.

In the seventeenth century, perhaps one of the saddest in our history, each one of us can view the conflict according to his sympathies or prejudices. Was it a Parliament representing a few rich men, the Pyms and Hampdens, who obstinately refused to tax themselves even for policies they supported; who demanded foreign adventure but refused supply; who living inland took no interest in the Navy and hence declined ship-money; or who having engrossed the great wealth of the nation refused to pay direct taxation and demanded that all imposts should fall upon the mass consumer?

Alternatively, was it a struggle where the Crown was claiming unreasonable and tyrannical rights, disruptive of parliamentary freedom, and ultimately leading to the establishment of a central government in England, not dissimilar to that being established in France and already operating in Spain? At any rate, it was a struggle of interests. It may perhaps be claimed that after the unhappy experience of the Civil War, the Cromwellian dictatorship, and the Restoration, our ancestors who made the bloodless revolution of 1688 were able to establish a workable compromise. Yet in effect it left the great power not in the hands of the Crown but in the landed families and the great capitalists.

So one can pursue the story. The gradual rise of the industrial and commercial classes, the battle of the Reform Bill, the transfer of power in the nineteenth century, first to the middle classes and thus to urban and rural workers, although still leaving great influence in the old governing class; and then after the First War the institution for the first time of something like a real democracy with almost universal suffrage. This led to the growth of Left-Wing thought and opinion, and after the Second War, under favourable economic conditions, the development of the trade unions as the striking force, so the Left would have it, of the labouring classes, leading to Socialism, or Communism.

Thus all through English history we have seen a struggle for dominance between different forces. Yet broadly there has been a traditional support for the Crown, the Government, Parliament, or whatever body could claim to be acting on behalf of general and not of sectional interests. Thus it is that Labour Governments largely relying on trade union funds with the mechanism of the Labour Party inextricably intertwined with that of the trade union structure, finds itself facing the old question – who governs? Governments, Parliament, or an outside body claiming considerable exception from the law, a privileged position, a replica in economic terms of the Medieval Church?

CHAPTER NINE

The Whig Tradition

IF the question had been posed only a few months ago, 'What was Whiggery and who were the Whigs?' not many people would have been able to give more than a vague answer. No doubt some recent students, fresh from school or university, might have fared better. But now, after the television version of Trollope's great series of political novels, everybody knows who were the Pallisers with the Duke of Omnium at their head. (Incidentally it is not altogether discouraging to realise how quickly an established instrument of authority can wither away and be forgotten. Perhaps in another hundred years an equal bewilderment would be caused by the question, 'What was the T.U.C.?'). Of course Trollope presented a picture of the Whigs at the end or near the end of their long tenure of power, just as Gibbon only skirted over the period of Augustus and his immediate successors in order to justify his title *Decline and Fall*.

Yet for nearly two centuries, from the revolution of 1688 until the formation of Mr Gladstone's Government of 1868, Whigs and Whiggery dominated English parliamentary and political life. It is true that the rise of the younger Pitt – the true founder of the second Tory Party – and the long Napoleonic Wars together with the fear of revolution after the peace made a long gap, during which the Tory Party recovered and held power, while the Whigs were split between the followers of the Duke of Portland and those of Fox. Nevertheless, with the Reform Bill of 1832, the power of the great Whig families (the Venetian oligarchy, as Disraeli called them) was restored and remained dominant until the rise of the Liberal Party after Palmerston's death. Thus, from 1688 to 1868, with a long interval, Whigs and Whiggery were in effective control.

Whiggery really meant the great families, Russells, Cavendishes, Bentincks, Spencers, Pelhams, Egertons, Grosvenors and all the rest. Although they took pride in what they called 'the Glorious Revolution', it was a very patrician and rather tame affair by modern standards. Many of its supporters came from Cavalier families, who had sacrificed for Charles I their fortunes and their lives in the Civil War. But they could not stomach the politics or the religion of James II. Both as strong Protestants and believers in the liberties, if not of the people, at any rate of the ruling class against the engrossing power of the royal prerogative they determined to call a halt. Thus the decisive invitation to William of Orange to come over and promote his dual claim as a supporter of 'Liberty' and as the husband of the King's elder daughter. So the Whigs had it both ways. They could boast of their Liberal tradition and think of themselves as Roman patriots. But they remained monarchists. Moreover it had all been done in a very quiet way, at any rate in England, with scarcely any fighting; for John Churchill changed sides and James II was amiable enough to seize upon the opportunities afforded him to escape to France. At the same time, while cherishing these libertarian traditions, the Whig dynasts could enjoy large rent-rolls and live in splendid Palladian houses in the middle of extensive parks.

Many of these imposing monuments to the Whig tradition have already disappeared. No doubt within another generation the rest will go. A few of the noblest may survive as public institutions, but their savour will have passed. They will be mere museums from which the spirit has fled. There was something peculiar about a Whig house and a certain similarity between them. The black and white marble hall; the painted ceiling; the Roman busts; the pictures which several generations of young noblemen had brought back from their European tours (then a necessary part of education); the fine library, and a certain air of distinction. On the

Castle Howard: a perfect Whig habitat

whole the Whigs were the rich, the proud, the elite, and in many cases, the enlightened. They had not the dislike of 'trade' which pervaded the Tory nobility and gentry. Indeed they were the keen exploiters of their properties; coal mines, lead mines, quarries, canals and harbours. Moreover, it was the Whigs who were the great travellers, and with their long purses brought from Italy, and later France, countless artistic treasures – statues, well-heads, carpets, tapestries, pictures, drawings, books and furniture. All this is now called, quaintly enough, 'our national heritage'.

With the exception of the short period when Harley and Bolingbroke seized power from Marlborough and Godolphin – those fateful years – the Whigs were broadly dominant from the Revolution of 1688 until 1783. In that year the cynical coalition between Lord North and Fox shocked even hardened politicians. But it was not long before, with the King's ardent support, the younger Pitt began his long rule. The French Revolution; the Napoleonic Wars; the split in the Whig party, involving the tragic end to the long friendship between Burke and Fox – all this led to the emergence of what has been called 'the second Tory party'. For nearly a hundred years the Whigs had ruled, and only the genius of Pitt, although of Whig descent, could construct a party out of the depressed and divided Tories.

When the tide turned, in 1830, leading to the first Reform Bill in 1832, the old Whig authority returned, based partly on Whig principles and partly on Whig influence. Although it yielded to Liberalism in 1868, yet it lasted, in one form or another, till the opening years of the twentieth century.

Naturally some of the great nobles were still Tories, but their strength had been weakened. On the whole the Tories were to be found among the squires (whether of the Western or the Allworthy type), the one-thousand to two-thousand-acre men. They were split between those who accepted the Hanoverian succession, with different degrees of resignation, and those who still hankered after the Stuarts.

The Jacobites were strong in certain parts of the country, especially in the north-west, but like all revolutionary or semi-revolutionary parties were always under a cloud. It was the policy of the Whigs from Walpole afterwards to accuse even loyal Tories of being Jacobites in disguise. During the eighteenth century there were, of course, divisions and rivalries; but these were not 'party' disputes in the modern sense, they were internal jealousies between whig groups and families. Their prestige was easily restored when the party returned to office united after a gap of forty years to carry, some of them reluctantly, some enthusiastically, the Reform Bill of 1832. Naturally there were many Whigs, especially the more recently risen families like the Lambs (of whom Melbourne was the head) who shrank from anything approaching democracy. Melbourne was as hostile to such a concept as Palmerston. But at the same time the tradition of what would now be called 'advanced' opinion was by no means negligible and encouraged by such men as Lord Shelburne, afterwards Lord Lansdowne. Moreover, the great Whig hero, Charles James Fox, was a truly popular leader, in Parliament and outside.

There was always, therefore, a mixed stream in the Whig tradition, just as in French opinion in the eighteenth century. If there were few Whig sympathisers with Rousseau, there were many Voltaireans.

Readers, and now 'viewers', of Trollope will have enjoyed a wonderfully accurate and acute picture of the last stages of Whig dominance. The author, with his usual subtlety and delicacy of observation has given a remarkable portrayal of Whiggery just before the beginning of its 'decline and fall'. The aloofness and arrogance of the Duke of Omnium, the shyness and pride of 'Planty Pal', the solid good sense of the Duke of St Bungay, are admirably portrayed. Indeed all the little characteristics of the Whig are beautifully painted.

Although after 1868 a Liberal Government can be said to have superseded the old Whig Governments, yet the Whigs, though merged with the Liberals, by no means lost their identity. Mr Gladstone became Prime Minister for the first time after the General Election of November 1868. In his Cabinet of fifteen members, Lord Hatherley, Earl de Grey (afterwards Marquis of Ripon), the Earl of Kimberley, the Earl of Clarendon, Earl Granville, the Duke of Argyll, the Marquess of Hartington were Whigs; and grand Whigs. Indeed there was no one in this Cabinet who could be called radical, except Mr Bright. Curiously enough, Gladstone always described this Cabinet as the best instrument to carry on public affairs with which he had ever been connected. The Cabinet of 1880 formed after the fall of Lord Beaconsfield's great Administration was equally aristocratic – Lord Spencer, the Duke of Argyll, Sir William Harcourt, Lord Granville, Lord Kimberley, Lord Hartington – these all came from leading Whig families. The only representative of the old radicalism was Mr Bright and of the new radicalism, Mr Joseph Chamberlain. It will be seen therefore how strong was the grasp on power of the Whig grandees. This was due to Mr Gladstone himself; for he had more confidence in the Whigs than in the rising Liberals. The long Whig ascendancy was at last to come to an end by Mr Gladstone's own action. For it was on the issue of Home Rule for Ireland in 1886 that the Whigs were fatally divided. Mr Gladstone's decision, taken so suddenly, without consultation with his colleagues, and announced so strangely by what we should now call 'a leak' (Herbert Gladstone's famous Hawarden kite) offended the graver Whigs, many of whom had an unhappy experience of his last Government, dogged by so many disasters. The announcement was like a flash of lightning, and rent the Whigs as it might have split an ancient oak in one of their great parks.

Thus, while many remained loyal to Gladstone and Liberalism, others drifted into Liberal Unionism and gradually in the process of time (but quite a long time) became united with the Conservative Party. Yet even in his fourth Cabinet formed in 1892 after the schism, the well-known Whig names are not absent – Kimberley, Harcourt, Rosebery, Ripon, Spencer. Although there were now more representatives of middle-class Liberalism and radicalism, yet there were still the great Whig figures. Even in the families which had parted from Gladstone, like the Cavendishes, the tradition was not altogether lost. For instance, my father-in-law, afterwards 9th Duke of Devonshire, stood for West Derbyshire

Gladstone's first Cabinet, 1868

Hatherley, Cardwell, Lowe, Clarendon, De Grey, Granville, Fortescue, Childers, Bruce, Goschen, Gladstone, Bright, Argyll, Kimberley, Hartington

Gladstone's Cabinet, 1880

Northbrook, Dodson, Harcourt, Kimberley, Hartington, Argyll, Spencer, Selborne, Chamberlain, Childers, Gladstone, Bright, Granville, Forster.

and sat in the House of Commons for many years as a 'Liberal anti-Gladstonian'. This clumsy name shows how strongly he and his friends stuck by their attachment to the word Liberal. His younger brother, Richard Cavendish, remained with his party, and in the General Election of 1906 stood as a Liberal candidate under Campbell-Bannerman's leadership. Lady Frederick Cavendish the heroic widow of the Chief Secretary for Ireland, who was stabbed to death in Phoenix Park, Dublin, remained a loyal Liberal and a life-long Home Ruler. This recalls to me a most dramatic election story. A meeting at Bakewell was being held at the General Election which followed the Home Rule split in 1886. The Liberal candidate was attacking (and quite fairly) the desertion of the Cavendish interest. 'Since when,' he cried, 'have the colours of Cavendish been changed from yellow to blue?' It was a meeting largely of tenant farmers or employees on the Chatsworth Estate. A voice called out from the back of the hall, 'Since they were dyed in the blood of Lord Frederick Cavendish.' This so excited the audience that they advanced upon the platform and threw the candidate into the river. Happily he was revived by the latest methods of the great Dr Sylvester; but he lost the seat.

Owing to the Liberal, and later Liberal Unionist sympathies of my parents, they had more friends in these groups than among the Tories. My mother was brought into contact with many leading Whigs after 1886. Indeed, one of my godfathers – Lord Carlisle – was the head of one of the great branches of the Howard family, with a long tradition of service to the Whig party. Castle Howard and Naworth were important in the political life of the north. My godmother, Lady Arthur Russell, was married to a brother of the Duke of Bedford, with all that the name of Russell means over many generations. (By a strange irony, Lady Arthur was a Frenchwoman, daughter of M. de Peyronnet, whose ultra-reactionary views helped to bring about in 1830 the fall of his master Charles X.) It was not therefore altogether a surprise to me when I married into a Whig family in 1920 to find various traces of these old feelings. It was perhaps something like the sympathy between boys who had been at the same school, although their ways may have parted in after life. Thus Whigs retained a sense of something which bound them together which they did not feel towards their Tory friends, however much they admired them. Lord Hartington (later 8th Duke of Devonshire) had never felt quite at ease with Lord Salisbury. On the other hand, Lord Crewe and Lord Spencer, who stuck to the Liberal Party, were among my father-in-law's most intimate friends. These sympathies were perhaps strengthened because the Whigs continued their Erastian and mildly anti-clerical tradition. Tories were apt to be High Churchmen, which no Whig, I think, can ever have been. Indeed it was Mr Gladstone's Toryism which had been the basis of the strong Church views which he cherished to the end, somewhat to the surprise, and even dismay, of his Liberal and Radical colleagues.

Up to the First War Whigs remained prominent in spite of the schism. The great Lord Rosebery, one of the richest as well as one of the most erudite and eloquent men in the whole country, had retired in the closing years of the century into a sort of independent position, drawing away from the radical element in the Liberal Party. Yet he was a deeply respected figure and acted almost as the 'public orator' of Britain. Lord Crewe was the minister whom Asquith most trusted and consulted with the greatest confidence. Lord Elgin, Lord Ripon and Lord Carrington were in his Government. The Spencers, the Harcourts and the Greys as well as the Russells, kept their Whiggism pure. Sir Edward Grey who was Foreign Secretary from 1906 to 1916 was a typical Whig. From the public gallery I heard his 'winding up' speech in the debate that followed the report of the Marconi Committee where the conduct of the two leading Ministers, Lloyd George and Isaacs (afterwards Lord Reading), was described in a way which if it acquitted them of any malfeasance could not fail to comment on a certain lack of candour. Sir Edward Grey's cool, dignified and somewhat haughty reply to the Tory critics showed his loyalty to his friends, combined with a kind of disdainful disgust with the whole affair.

Political Whiggery might almost be said to have ended with the

First World War; the last of the great Whig figures to make a striking impact was Lord Lansdowne. I remember him very well, for he was my wife's grandfather and we were married from Lansdowne House, (Devonshire House having already been condemned). It was a wonderful house although on a much smaller scale than its neighbour. It had all the right things in the way of pictures and furniture, especially French furniture. He also had, as every Whig nobleman in principle should possess, a statue gallery with some exquisite examples brought over at different times in the eighteenth century. He had married a Tory wife, a Hamilton, and was sometimes rather distressed by his brothers-in-law, whom he thought boisterous and almost vulgar. I remember being deeply touched when after a family dinner party he, a former Governor-General of Canada, a former Viceroy of India, a former Secretary of State for War, the Foreign Secretary who had brought about the *Entente Cordiale* with France, actually wrote a letter to me, a young man just engaged to his granddaughter, apologizing for some conversation at his dinner table that he thought might have offended me. Lord Lansdowne was perhaps the last and most typical of his kind. He was small, with beautiful hands and feet and showed something of his French blood. (He was descended from the Comte de Flahaut, Napoleon's aide-de-camp and a considerable figure in French history.) Born in 1845 he was already seventy when he took office for the last time in Asquith's first coalition Government in 1915. Before it broke up to make way for Lloyd George's War Government of 1916, Lord Lansdowne had formed doubts on two supreme issues; first as to the ability of Britain and her then allies to bring a war against Germany to a successful conclusion and secondly (and more important) as to the possibility of any ordered and tolerable world surviving the frightful calamity of a fight to the finish. Hence the famous Lansdowne letter to the *Daily Telegraph* in November 1917, pleading for an attempt to seek a settlement by negotiation. This action was admired by some, deplored by more. To members of his own family and circle it was a bitter blow, since they were all, in one way or another, serving in the war. Indeed, Lord Lansdowne's

Lord Lansdowne with Maurice Macmillan

younger son had already been killed. To many others either with longer views or more peaceful inclinations it came as a welcome signal of hope. At any rate Lord Lansdowne with his immense prestige and long service could not be accused of lack of patriotism. He was loyal to the oldest tradition of his upbringing. Some viewed his action more in sorrow than in anger. Others thought of it as a tremendous demonstration of the traditional sanity and wisdom which he had inherited from his great ancestor, Lord Shelburne, who after the final fall of Lord North was responsible for the peace which brought to an end the American War of Independence.

Yet Lord Lansdowne had long been and still was leader of the Conservative Party in the House of Lords, just as Bonar Law was leader of the party in the Commons. There was no leader of the whole party appointed between the resignation of Mr Balfour in 1912 and the acceptance by Bonar Law of office as Prime Minister in 1922. It was not a leadership but a consulship.

I remember a story told me by the Duke of Devonshire which was very typical of Lord Lansdowne. The Duke had succeeded in 1909, much to his disgust, for he had to leave the House of Commons of which he had been a Member for many years. He then became a Whip in the House of Lords, under Lord Lansdowne's leadership, the Conservative and Unionist Party being in opposition. One day they were walking back from the House of Lords on what had seemed a brilliant, warm, sunny afternoon. The House had risen early. It was about five o'clock. They were accoutred in the uniform of the day – frock-coat, top-hat, walking-stick. Suddenly a terrible storm came on, with drenching rain. They had no protection. When they got to the top of the Duke of York steps, the Duke said to his father-in-law, 'Let's get into the Carlton Club, out of this drenching rain.' (The old Carlton Club before its destruction by bombing in the Second World War stood next to the Reform, in Pall Mall.) Lord Lansdowne looked at him with horror. Although he had resigned from a Liberal Government in 1873, held the highest office in successive Unionist Governments and was now the actual leader of the Unionist Party in the Upper House, such a proposal was most distasteful to him. The Duke told me that Lord Lansdowne gave him the kind of look as if he had suggested something utterly disgraceful or as if he had committed some unforgivable act. 'What do you mean, Victor, go in here? Not at all.' Drenched as they were, he insisted on walking all the way along Pall Mall, up St James's Street, until they got to Brooks's Club. Here was a Whig Club, where the portrait of Charles James Fox still presided over a collection of noblemen and gentlemen, some still working with the Liberal Party, some

with the Conservatives, but all by adoption or inheritance undoubted Whigs. My father-in-law maintained some of the same
prejudices which became more apparent after his illness when he
had less control of his temper. I remember his calling out once on
a grouse moor, protesting against 'these damned grouse; they
won't fly straight – like a lot of Tories'.

In more serious matters the Duke remained a true Liberal.
During his tenure of the Colonial Office in 1923 he left his mark
upon British colonial policy by the famous declaration of 'para-
mountcy' in East Africa. This formally declared that on any
question which might arise where the interests of the settlers and
the native inhabitants were in conflict those of the latter must be
regarded as 'paramount'. At that time this doctrine, if not revolutionary, was certainly unexpected. Although great pressure
was brought upon him to withdraw or amend this declaration he
remained quite firm and could not be shaken either by his colleagues
or by his advisers.

What had been the secret of this strange tradition and by what
means were a few families and their relatives or adherents able to
play so great a part in our history for so long a period? Broadly
'The Glorious Revolution' of 1688 was brought about by certain
Whig families who could not stomach the political and ecclesiastical
aberrations of James II. With the new regime their power and
influence grew strong, although William III tried to create what
would now be called a 'bi-partisan executive'.

As the pressure of the war with France grew greater, the
Government fell into wholly Whig hands. Bolingbroke and Harley
only seized it for a moment to arrange a peace for which, however
disgraceful the Whigs may have thought it, the country was
yearning. After the Treaty of Utrecht and the death of Queen
Anne, the succession of Hanoverian monarchs began, and a
few families were able to seize power and parcel it out amongst
themselves. Indeed the history of eighteenth-century politics is
really only the history of the warring clans among the Whigs,
followers of Walpole, followers of Newcastle, followers of Mr
Pelham, followers of the Duke of Bedford, the Cavendish interest

and so forth. Only the formation of the Younger Pitt's Government in 1783 led to the exclusion of the Whigs for forty years. Yet this was essentially an interlude. Meanwhile it was Whig pressure that brought about Catholic Emancipation, and it was Whig influence that in the end destroyed the successors of Canning. From the first Reform Bill of 1832 until 1868 politics was largely controlled by the Whigs. The normal Government was of course a sort of unofficial coalition. The Tories, the true Tories, the old protectionist party now led by the brilliant Benjamin Disraeli, could seldom quite reach a working majority in the House of Commons against the groups opposed to it. These consisted of Whigs, Liberals, Radicals, Peelites and what was known as the Irish Brigade. So long as these strangely ill-assorted groups could be kept in line, a Whig Government, organised and managed by a great Whig nobleman, could be confirmed in office. Most of Disraeli's efforts during this period were directed to seducing one or other from their loyalty to this ill-assorted combination. When he did so, a Whig Government would fall, but a Tory Government – being in a minority – would seldom last for more than a year or fifteen months, sometimes less. Incidentally, it should be remembered that Disraeli succeeded in carrying the second Reform Bill, with all its intricacies, in a House where there was no closure and no guillotine, where every detail of every amendment was discussed at length, through an assembly in which he stood in a minority of seventy or more.

Even after the death of Palmerston and the forming of Parties into more coherent groups under the new gladiators, Gladstone and Disraeli, the Whigs were still great figures, as shown by the composition of Liberal Cabinets where they enjoyed an authority far above their numerical importance. Of course by their wide properties they had considerable influence both in the rural areas and in some of the boroughs which they still more or less controlled. Since, unlike the Tory squires, the Whig grandees were great men for money, they were indeed the entrepreneurs of the nineteenth century. The Egertons built the Bridgwater Canal, the Cavendishes built Barrow-in-Furness with its steelworks and shipyard, Buxton, Eastbourne, and a great part of the railways in Southern Ireland. Thus while the Whigs on the one side were old-fashioned and held themselves rather aloof in their dignity, on the other they adopted with keenness modern notions and modern inventions. In this sense they were what would now be called 'tycoons'.

It was not perhaps until 1917, with the failure of the last great Whig's final appeal for peace, that the Whig influence as such came to an end. It was a strange but not inglorious story. It had lasted in one form or another for two hundred and thirty years. It began with a protest against extremism – political or religious. It ended with a dignified but fruitless appeal for moderation. It is perhaps worth thinking what kind of a world it might have been, certainly what kind of Europe it might have been, if Lord Lansdowne had found followers in all the countries, and the First World War had ended in 1916 or 1917 before Europe had torn herself fatally asunder and before the New World was brought in to decide the fate of the Old World, to resolve the immediate contest, and then by withdrawal into isolation to abandon the bruised and bleeding nations. At the time I, like all the young men who fought in the war, viewed with distaste Lord Lansdowne's intervention. When I got to know him later I could not but admire the courage and dignity of this old man who had done what he knew would be repudiated by most of his friends and relations, not because he thought that it was a spectacular gesture or to salve the wounds of his own heart, but carefully, precisely, in good order, because he thought that it was his duty.

CHAPTER TEN

Independent Members

WHEN I was first elected to the House of Commons in 1924 the party system was almost fully developed. It was sustained by a powerful apparatus of Whips in the House, and an elaborate organisation outside. Yet it was not able to impose a complete or rigid authority upon Members of the House of Commons to the extent that has since been common practice. There are many reasons for this. The very large Conservative majorities in 1924, 1931 and even 1935 gave more freedom to individual Members and groups of Members to produce ideas and even programmes of their own without jeopardising the life of the Government to which they gave a general support. Thus the various parliamentary bodies with which I was associated could promote policies in opposition to, or at least in advance of, the official view. The Young Conservatives included Oliver Stanley, John Loder (afterwards Lord Wakehurst), Bob Boothby and myself as its core; we were sometimes ridiculed, sometimes admired and sometimes feared. But we had a definite position which was recognised. The northern group, representing particularly the constituencies most affected by the industrial depression, exercised considerable influence. Other combinations of Members came into being, which attracted support not merely among the 'young and irresponsible' – the words normally used by older people about the coming generation – but from respected statesmen when they happened to be out of office. On social questions Conservatives like Nancy Astor, Lord Henry Bentinck, Sir Robert Newman and many others could be relied on to harass the Government when they seemed to be inactive or obstructive.

But this independence could not merely be attributed to the size of the majority and the greater freedom which resulted. At that time, many Members of the Conservative Party, perhaps the majority, had no desire at all for political advancement. A large number, young and old, had come into the House of Commons as their fathers and grandfathers had done, from a general feeling that it was the right way to serve their country and especially the localities in which they lived. It was quite remarkable how many constituencies, sometimes boroughs but more usually counties, had a long record of electing men of the same family, generation after generation. These were generally men of independent means as well as of independent ideas. They were loyal but not subservient to Ministers. Sometimes, when roused, they were rude to them. I have never forgotten how Sidney Herbert, a most respected example of this type of Member turned on Neville Chamberlain after Munich not merely with anger but with contempt. There were also Members chiefly occupied by their own careers in business or at the bar. Indeed in view of the small remuneration between the wars, there was no particular inducement to enter the House of Commons or even seek Ministerial office as a career or 'for profit'. Men like Sir John Simon and other leading barristers could earn immense sums, as yet subjected to only moderate taxation, by pursuing their own professions. Thus the Government had always to be careful lest it offend individuals or groups which could be led but not driven.

One of the most characteristic of this traditional type was Lord Henry Bentinck, who had sat for Nottingham for many years where he was always honoured and sometimes feared. I always felt that he must have inherited some of the characteristics of Lord George Bentinck, Disraeli's friend and mentor. By all the rules he was a bad speaker, unable to produce his voice effectively and waving his arms with a strange pumping movement, as we are told Lord George was apt to do. Yet on the rare occasions when he took part in debate he was singularly impressive. He denounced, with a combination of aristocratic scorn and democratic fervour, those whom he suspected of obstructing the particular social reforms in which he was specially interested. At one time I remember he was obsessed by the danger of white lead, and it was largely through the agitation of Lord Henry and his friends that the necessary legislation was passed to regulate its use. A very handsome man himself, he was married to one of the most beautiful women in England. Lord and Lady Henry made a most impressive couple, splendid hosts at their home in Underley on the River Lune, and particularly kind to the younger generation. He was a man of amiable but explosive character. On one occasion he was determined to leave the Chamber rather than support the Government in a course which he thought mean and reactionary; it had something to do with a Factory Bill. Passing out of the Members' Lobby he was stopped by the Whip on the door who was trying to keep a House. Lord Henry attacked him in the most violent language which echoed down the various corridors and even startled the police. (I remember my wife telling me that when they were children and the Yeomanry were encamped in Chatsworth Park their governess insisted that the schoolroom should be moved to another side of the house lest she and her sisters should be contaminated by the expressions used by Lord Henry while drilling his troops.) At any rate, on this occasion, as he was going through the Cloister to get his hat and stick, he reflected that it was hard upon the Whip, who bore no responsibility for the particular decision to which Lord Henry objected, to be attacked in this violent way. He came back all the way up the stairs to apologise; but in the course of his apology he lost his temper again, attacked the Whip even more fiercely, leaving this astonished junior member of the Administration appalled by this second and quite uncalled-for flow of recrimination. If Lord Henry was what would now be called 'a special case' there were at that time many others not so eccentric but nevertheless equally independent. It was amongst these that I used in my rebel days to seek out allies.

There were in addition the University Members, only abolished in 1948 by the Labour Government which followed the Second

A. P. Herbert and Sir Arthur Salter

War. Although it could certainly be argued that the University seats had sometimes been misused, as a refuge for important Conservatives who had been defeated in an Election, yet on the whole they brought into the House some unusual characters, who added to our pleasure and instruction. Professor Oman never lost an occasion to deplore the debasement of the currency. He did not object to the issue of banknotes, which he thought anyway contemptible. It was the new silver coins, with some strange alloy which turned them yellow. These raised his indignation to a point of frenzy. Nor should the name of Alan Herbert – my old Oxford friend in pre-1914 days – be forgotten. He was not only a wit, but a reformer. Nor should the services to social reform on many fronts given by Miss Rathbone be unrecorded. She was a noble representative of an old Victorian tradition. Perhaps the two most distinguished University Members during my whole time in the House were Sir John Anderson and Sir Arthur Salter. The first was elected for the Scottish Universities on his return from the governorship of Bengal just before the Second World War. His part in the war is well known. But only those who saw him at work can understand the importance of his contribution. He remained 'independent' in mind and spirit until he left the House of Commons for good in 1950. The second was Sir Arthur Salter (now Lord Salter) one of the best and most practical of economists, who was both respected and loved by all who enjoyed his friendship. Moderate and persuasive in debate, rapid and effective in administration, he was in every sense a great public servant.

On the Labour side the Opposition being smaller was more cohesive. Nevertheless there was the famous Clydeside group, members of the old Independent Labour Party. The story of this party is not without interest. Founded in 1893, it was one of the original bodies forming the Labour Representative Committee in 1900. Although affiliated to the Labour Party, it retained its identity. In the 1920s differences grew acute, and among the 288 'Labour' Members elected in 1929 only some 37 belonged to the I.L.P. In 1932 the I.L.P. was 'disaffiliated' but not utterly destroyed. For in 1935 17 I.L.P. candidates stood, all against official Labour candidates, and four were elected – all in Glasgow. After the Second War, the I.L.P. faded out. Nevertheless, although its body lies mouldering in the grave, its soul may perhaps be said to be marching on in the shape of the Tribune group.

During these years, before 1939, the Clydesiders like their successors in later times, sat below the gangway, and were organised into a separate body, like the old Fourth Party in the last century, of which Arthur Balfour was the most distinguished member. The ablest among them was undoubtedly J. Wheatley. His views were extreme, almost revolutionary; but he had great administrative capacity and was one of the best Ministers produced by the Labour Party. His early death was a great loss to his Party. As for the Conservatives, Wheatley would have sent us all to the guillotine (or so we thought); but he had a kindly look, with his eyes sparkling with apparent benignity behind his spectacles, not unlike Mr Pickwick in appearance. (I noticed the same characteristics in Mr Vyshinsky who although the brutal prosecutor of the Russian regime under Stalin, looked as if butter would not melt in his mouth.)

Of quite a different order was David Kirkwood. He had been a real revolutionary and had been sent to prison in the First War.

John Wheatley

David Kirkwood

George Buchanan

Campbell Stephen

But he mellowed rapidly, and although he talked a great deal of heady stuff in the Chamber he was a charming companion in the Smoking Room. Campbell Stephen, who could talk more or less indefinitely without either repeating himself or being dull or being 'called to order', used to delight me because he annoyed both front benches equally. In this, as a confirmed back-bencher, I took a malicious pleasure. Geordie Buchanan, who disguised under a somewhat guileless appearance a brilliant intellect, was half schoolboy, half rebel. He looked so innocent that his enemies declared he had started life as the decoy who wins the first few runs in the three-card trick or in thimblerig. But Jimmy Maxton was the king and leader of them all. Many descriptions of him have been written, but none can quite depict the strange and ominous appearance of this man. His long black hair, his sunken cheeks, his deep-set eyes, combined to make him look a true revolutionary. He seemed to have stepped straight out of the French Revolution. Listening to him denouncing the aristocrats – or their successors, the bourgeois classes – one felt that he would happily condemn us to the lamp-post or guillotine. But he had one fatal weakness; he was born with – or developed in the House of Commons, I know not which – a sense of humour. After a terrifying attack upon us all, he would join us in the Smoking Room in friendly conversation. I remember one of the stories that he told against himself. When he was in prison in the war, he had managed to converse, during the dreary tramp of the prisoners round the yard, with one or two of his fellow convicts. He asked what they were in for. One for housebreaking; one for manslaughter ('hit the old woman on the head with a bottle'); another for burglary with assault. When they found out, however, that Maxton was in for sedition, they made a formal protest to the Governor against having to associate with a man who was a traitor to his country.

When he spoke, the House filled up. However much many of our respectable and solid Members disapproved of him, they could not help being fascinated.

Most of us had a great regard for the Clydesiders, for they wanted

James Maxton

nothing for themselves and obtained nothing. Only Geordie Buchanan at the end of his career was given a post in the Public Assistance Board; this met with general approval. How the Clydesiders lived I do not know. Their material conditions must have involved great hardship; but they were sustained by their enthusiasm and by their humour. On our side of the House we liked them all the more because the conventional Labour Members so thoroughly disapproved of them.

The Liberals, whether Lloyd Georgians or Asquithians, constituted so small a party that they had little hope of returning to power. Their best chance would have been no doubt a balance between the Conservative and Labour forces, but even when this occurred to some extent in 1929 the Liberals so distrusted each other that they could achieve little. Apart from Lloyd George, who was a national rather than a party figure, the Liberals had many officers but few troops. Asquith had now retired to the House of Lords, and the two other leading Liberals, Simon and Samuel, distrusted each other as much as they feared Lloyd George. Lloyd George disliked Simon whom he regarded as a pedant. The fact that he was one of the most brilliant barristers of the day did not impress him. I remember him telling me that barristers were all right to plead in court, but seldom effective in the House of Commons and generally useless in Council. It was of Simon and his waverings between Right and Left that Lloyd George is supposed to have said, 'The Rt. Hon. Gentleman has sat so long upon the fence that the iron has entered into his soul.' Lloyd George equally disliked Samuel, with his prim precision and affectation of high moral principles. Nevertheless Samuel was an extremely able debater. He could dissect any subject to any degree, but he could never put it together again; so that at the end you were left in a state of bewildered depression.

My long years as a back-bench Member, some sixteen in all, were at least a good training. I knew from experience the sensitive relations between the Government and especially the Government Whips and the rank and file. It is very easy for Ministers, especially newly-appointed Ministers – or even in these days where everybody must have a title, for Shadow Ministers – to show a certain affectation of front-bench superiority towards the back-benches. This can easily become a cause of friction, even of bitterness. No one could feel this about our leader, Baldwin. If he seldom spoke to his followers, he sat in the House for hours and listened to their speeches. In the Smoking Room he would make friendly faces at them in his shy and unassuming way. But towards the young under-secretaries just risen from the ranks, we had the same kind of feeling as private soldiers towards newly promoted non-commissioned officers. The old man, the Colonel, was not so bad; but these corporals and sergeants were intolerable.

The new groupings which have formed themselves may have produced some new eccentrics, but I have not yet observed them, except perhaps, Mr Enoch Powell. So far neither the Scottish nor the Welsh Nationalists can boast anything to compare with the old Irish wit and fantasy or the persistent eloquence of the Clyde-sider. Yet however mechanical the procedure of Parilament may become with all the pressure on its time and the need to turn out legislation (including two or three Finance Bills a year) it will, I hope, always include a number of independent and irreverent figures. Unhappily, they tend to fade away. They either lose their seats from the pressure of the constituency machine or, worse still, are absorbed into the vast dullness of the administrative structure. For entertainment purposes, they disappear into the ranks of either ex-M.P.s or Ministers.

CHAPTER ELEVEN

Women in Politics

THE position of women in politics does not depend entirely upon their constitutional or Parliamentary rights. All through history the political power of women has been displayed sometimes openly, sometimes behind the scenes. Queens and courtiers, wives and mistresses, have at different stages all played dominant roles.

In the early years of the nineteenth century the great political hostesses, Georgiana, Duchess of Devonshire, Lady Melbourne, Lady Jersey and others, undoubtedly influenced the course of events, partly by the inspiration of their own circle and partly by skilful intrigue. In the middle of the century, there can be no doubt that the charm and exertions of Lady Palmerston did much to strengthen the authority of her husband by spreading his popularity throughout both political parties. Liberal in name, Conservative in policy, Palmerston was able, for a period of some ten years, to maintain his power partly by his personality, partly by the similarity of his approach to affairs with that of the ordinary middle-class voter of the day, and partly by the wide influence which Lady Palmerston exerted. At the end of the century the great houses, Whig and Tory, still had the means of rallying their partisans, largely by the influence of the gracious hospitality dispensed. Readers of the letters and memoirs of the time will recall the importance of the position of Teresa, Lady Londonderry, and Lady Salisbury, the Prime Minister's wife. At the beginning of the twentieth century the bitterness developed from the cruel events of the Boer War and the savage debates following Joseph

The Duchesses of Devonshire and Portland canvassing for votes
by Rowlandson

Chamberlain's great tariff campaign, were largely soothed by the personal friendships in the highest ranks of both sides. Balfour and Margot Tennant, later Mrs Asquith, were both members of that famous coterie that became known as the 'Souls'. Hostesses like Lady Desborough entertained their friends of both parties. This fact may have reduced their personal importance in any vital political issue. Nevertheless both directly by the influence of these well-known women on the social life of what would now be called the 'establishment' and indirectly through their influence on individual statesmen, it must be admitted that the effective power of women in politics did not depend on their formal admission to political rights.

One of the most remarkable instances of the influence of women in the old way – that is before their political rights were recognised – is to be found in the part played by Edie, Lady Londonderry, a leading Tory hostess, the daughter of one of the old Tory families through her father Harry Chaplin, and the wife of Lord Londonderry, a magnate of the old school. She became an intimate friend of Ramsay MacDonald, and many people believed that she had a great part in his decision to form the National Government of 1931. Whether this be true or exaggerated, she certainly did not need to be given a Parliamentary vote or be allowed to stand for the House of Commons to enhance her persuasive charm.

Following the Speaker's Conference, which represented all parties, by the Reform Bill of 1918 women of thirty years and over were granted the Parliamentary franchise. Members of all the political parties had previously been divided on this issue; but the war had an emotional as well as a logical effect upon the great changes embodied in the Act. This made an extension of the franchise on a scale that could not have been dreamt of in the pre-war years. For the first time, so far as the male population was concerned, something like complete democracy was established. The fact that the women's vote was restricted to the age of thirty and that plural voting, including the business vote, was retained up to 1948, hardly affected the issue. The figures speak for themselves. In 1910, when two General Elections were held on the

Women vote for the first time

gravest constitutional matters, the electorate consisted of some $7\frac{1}{2}$ million out of a population of some 26 million over the age of twenty-one. By 1919 it had risen to nearly 22 million out of an electorate of the same age to just over 27 million. By 1929, owing to Mr Baldwin's introduction of what was called the 'flapper' vote – that is by including women of twenty-one years of age – the electorate and the population over twenty-one had become almost identical.

The reasons which led after the First War to the introduction of women's franchise were based largely upon the novel social situation created by war conditions. Not only had women workers been employed through almost every factory in the country but they had invaded for the first time occupations which had always seemed unsuitable, such as the metal industries. In the vital production of munitions they had been able both to replace men drafted into the services and to fill the new munition factories which were necessary to produce armaments on an unprecedented scale. There had been nothing in our history equivalent to this complete mobilisation of the female population. It could no longer be argued that the woman's place was in the home, when she had taken her place so triumphantly in the factory or on the farm.

At the same time an almost equally spectacular development took place by the admission of women as candidates to the House of Commons. With the strange perversity which has pursued the impact of Ireland on the British House of Commons through many ages, the first woman to be elected in 1918 was the Countess Markievicz, who was returned for one of the Dublin Constituencies. She, however, with the rest of the Sinn Fein Members, refused to take her seat. It was thus Lady Astor who can claim to be the first woman actually to serve in the House of Commons. For four years she stood alone; and it was not until the Election of 1922 that she was joined by a colleague in the shape of Mrs Wintringham, a Liberal Member. Indeed up to the Second World War the women Members of the House of Commons were remarkably few. The actual numbers were as follows: two after the 1922 Election; eight at the 1923 Election; four in 1924; in 1929 the figure rose to

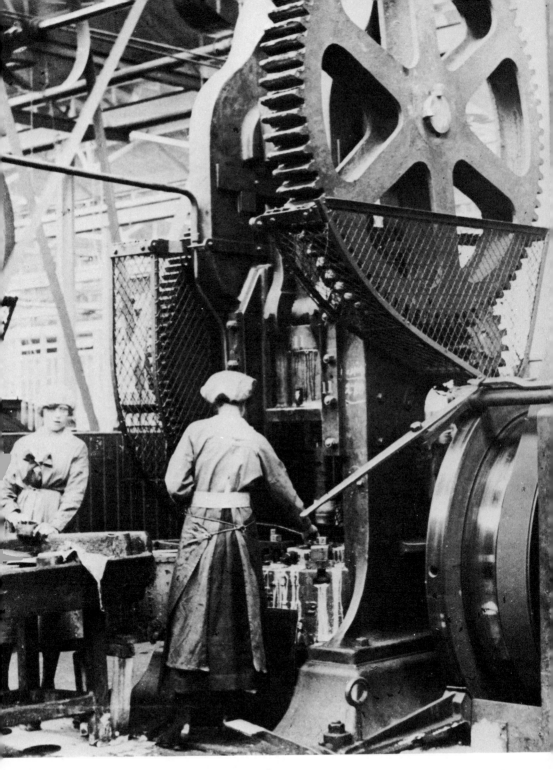

Women working in a shell factory, 1918

fourteen; in 1931 to fifteen; but in 1935 dropped again to nine.

It will be seen therefore that the woman Member of Parliament, in the period which I am describing, was indeed one of a very small band of pioneers. Even in the Election of 1966 they were less than thirty. Moreover it must be admitted that some of the earliest gained their positions by a sort of hereditary right. Lady Astor was elected at Plymouth, following her husband who had succeeded to his father's peerage. The Duchess of Atholl, the first woman M.P. in Scotland, could claim to be chieftainess of a great clan. Lady Iveagh, elected in 1927, again followed her husband at a by-election due to his succession to his father's earldom. Lady Cynthia Mosley, herself a woman of great gifts, depended for her success in 1929 largely upon her husband's reputation. Lady Noel-Buxton elected in 1930 enjoyed a similar advantage. This is equally true of Mrs Philipson, whose husband was unseated in 1923 on an election petition, as well as Lady Apsley who again followed her husband when he succeeded as Earl Bathurst in 1943.

Thus it will be seen that a high proportion of the few women who became Members of Parliament before the outbreak of the Second World War relied on the ability, popularity and general influence of that least attractive figure in feminist circles – a mere man and a mere husband. Even Megan Lloyd George, with all her high abilities, was supported by her father's fame. This was not true of the women who were elected on the Left – Miss Bond-field, Miss Susan Lawrence, Miss Jennie Lee, Mrs Manning and Miss Ellen Wilkinson. They stood and won in their own right. There were also some outstanding Conservatives, such as Miss Cazalet, Dame Florence Horsbrugh and Dame Irene Ward, who could make the same claim. There were also some notable Inde-pendents, such as Miss Rathbone.

Naturally so small a team was also select and individual. Many are alive who can still remember Lady Astor towards the end of her life. But few remain who can have a vivid memory of her in the period when she achieved this astonishing record. American by birth, wife of an American-born millionaire, whose father had achieved the unusual record of a reverse immigration, of extra-

Lady Astor

ordinarily vivid character, of great beauty, exerting over nearly all men and many women an indescribable but irresistible charm, Nancy Astor with her smart black tailored suit, white cuffs, white collar and tricorne hat, was certainly worthy of the novel part which a combination of chance and courage led her to play. Yet I am doubtful, in spite of my deep affection for her, whether her political power was much enhanced by her membership of the House of Commons. It was as a notable hostess, a lively character and above all a friend whose loyalty could be depended upon by every man and woman who needed her help, that she will be remembered and for which she was loved. Her interruptions in the House of Commons were often a source of confusion to her political friends rather than to her political enemies. She spoke with sincerity but without great power of argument or exposition. On the platform she had undoubtedly considerable effect; but here again she could be easily led into irrelevant or even irresponsible deviations. I remember her speaking once in Stockton-on-Tees to a great crowd of women. She certainly struck many happy notes, but there was

Conservative women M.P.s in 1931 : the Duchess of Atholl is in the centre of the front row

always some anxiety into what pitfall she might be enticed either by her own enthusiasm or by a well-timed interruption.

Edie, Lady Londonderry, Alice, Lady Salisbury, and perhaps Mrs Ronnie Greville, exercised more political power in the Conservative Party than Lady Astor achieved by her membership in the House of Commons. Indeed, busy as she was and devoted to her public duties, it was still at Cliveden surrounded by friends of all kinds and beloved equally by the old and the young that she shone. She had certainly a greater genius for friendship than for Parliamentary life.

On the other hand there were women on the Conservative side who won their positions, like any other Member of Parliament, by knowledge, intellectual capacity and hard work. A strange contrast to Lady Astor was the Duchess of Atholl, the Red Duchess as she was popularly known, owing to her sympathies with the legal Spanish Government in the Civil War. I was not infrequently in contact with her over various reforms in which we were jointly interested. She had a masculine mind with a notable academic record. Miss Horsbrugh, who became Minister for Education, would have won a place by right in any administration. Dame Irene Ward fought the Conservative cause on the north-east coast for nearly forty years and won a popularity in the House based upon

Megan Lloyd George   *Ellen Wilkinson*   *Jennie Lee and Aneurin Bevan*

her complete independence and lack of any unreasonable respect for Ministers. Among the Independents Miss Rathbone represented the old tradition of Liberal philanthropy. On the Labour side who can forget Jennie Lee, a miner's daughter, with her intellectual and rhetorical capacity combined with beauty and charm, or Miss Ellen Wilkinson with her startling and sometimes ferocious earnestness. Miss Bondfield, who became Minister of Labour in 1929, was unfortunate in being caught up in the terrible net of unemployment insurance and all its intricacies and anomalies – the dole as it was popularly but unfairly known. The most formidable of all in my recollection was Miss Susan Lawrence, masculine in the ordinary accepted sense both in intellect and character. She was the most dangerous opponent to challenge in the House, for she always knew the answer; and when she decided to stand against me at Stockton in 1935 I was much concerned. She was a good candidate, but on conventional lines. As a Minister, she had capacity of a very high order. It would not be right to omit from special mention in her own right, the most attractive of all Parliamentary figures – Megan Lloyd George.

There were many in this small band who made a considerable impression upon their fellow Members, and some I can see vividly before me. But I cannot honestly say that in my view they made any special contribution as women. As Members of Parliament they played their part, and considering that they were a select team it was no small part. But, with a few exceptions, they played it as Members and not as women. Some might have had even greater power outside the House of Commons.

Parliament soon got used to women Members, and although they treated them with courtesy they gave them no particular advantage, nor indeed did these ladies claim any. They were a notable band of pioneers, but even by the Second War they had ceased to be unique. They were treated primarily as Members of Parliament and not as women. Whether women liked being treated like this I do not know.

If the admission of women to the House of Commons was the product of the first War Coalition in 1918, their admission to the House of Lords can be claimed for a Conservative administration. I was Prime Minister when the Life Peerages Act of 1958 was passed and this enabled me in addition to introducing women into the Second Chamber on the same basis as men, at the same time to confer life peerages upon distinguished peeresses in their own right who were until then excluded. These included such well-known personalities as Lady Ravensdale, Lord Curzon's eldest daughter, who had inherited much of her father's ability as well as a hereditary peerage; and also Lady Ruthven, equally well-known as Lady Monckton, the wife of one of my oldest Oxford friends. This Act was completed in 1963 by the admission as of right of hereditary peeresses. In many ways the contribution of women to the House of Lords has been at least as great as that to the Commons. Moreover, the new senate (for that is what the House of Lords is rapidly becoming) is all the time gaining in authority while the House of Commons, in the opinion of many, seems to be declining.

Now, of course, a much more spectacular event has taken place which would have been quite inconceivable in the past. Nobody can maintain that the Conservative Party is hidebound or conventional in its choice of leaders. One hundred and thirty years ago, in a period of overwhelming defeat, the country gentlemen of England chose, somewhat unexpectedly, a brilliant but dandified

Jew, known as the author of some remarkable social and political novels and as an orator who had helped to destroy one of the most powerful Prime Ministers in history, Sir Robert Peel. Now the Conservative Party of today, widely based and drawn from every walk of life, has chosen a clever and attractive lady in somewhat similar conditions. *Prosit omen.*

Disraeli

Margaret Thatcher

CHAPTER TWELVE

Desperate Remedies

I

'ENGLAND does not like coalitions.' This famous dictum of Disraeli's has generally been accepted without demur. What he had in mind, when he made this aphorism, was the kind of combination of parties, without any fixed purpose or any coherent policy, whose sole object was to secure office for themselves and to deny access to power to their main opponents. Such was the hated Fox–North Coalition of 1783. A similar coalition was to lead the country – or rather drift with the country – into the Crimean War. To coalitions of this kind he rightly attributed confusion of method and infirmity of purpose.

Disraeli himself took part in no such administration. He twice served in, or presided over, minority governments, when his party had to depend on the good-will or exhaustion of the parties opposed to him. But he never entered a coalition.

On the other hand, a coalition – or combination – of parties and party leaders, commanding either the whole or the overwhelming majority of parliamentary and national assent; and formed to meet a special and perilous situation, should be judged by altogether different tests. During the hundred years from the Treaty of Vienna in 1815 to the outbreak of the First World War in 1914, the British people were fortunate enough never to be faced with any such overwhelming crisis as to require the cessation of all party divisions, and the concentration of the national unity of purpose under a national leadership.

We, in this twentiety century of 'progress' have been less

fortunate. In my lifetime four such coalitions or 'National Governments' have been formed under the harsh pressure of events – three under the strain of war and one before the threat, or what seemed the threat, of financial and economic collapse. Since it is not impossible that another of these critical moments in the life of the nation may recur, it is perhaps worth while considering these precedents.

Mr Asquith's Liberal Government, in spite of its brilliant membership, could not sustain the stress of war for more than a year. Somewhat reluctantly, under the dual pressure of Admiral Lord Fisher's resignation and the scandal of the shell shortage, he was forced to admit at least a fair proportion of Conservatives into his administration. Many of these individually he found agreeable companions, such as Balfour, Curzon, Crawford and Lansdowne. With Bonar Law, for whom he had an intellectual contempt, he was not so happy. When Asquith fell in December 1916 a truly national coalition was formed by Lloyd George, drawing support from Conservatives, Liberals and Labour, as well as introducing prominent and more or less non-party figures from industry and commerce. To this impressive team there was added the widely respected personality of General Smuts.

I was in hospital when this took place and still suffering severely from my wounds on the Somme; but I remember well the excitement caused among the officers and staff and the general sense of relief. We all felt that at last a more effective instrument of government had come into being and one more truly representative of the whole nation. Some of us, who had been fortunate to survive the first two years of war, may have hoped that the new Government might be able to exercise some restraint upon the generals, especially the High Command, with their insatiable appetitite for grandiose attacks upon the German lines, involving immense losses and puny gains. Alas, we were too confident. Lloyd George, with all his courage and ingenuity, was never able to impose his authority on the soldiers, who were as skilful and unscrupulous in defending their position as was any politician in attacking it. Hence, a year later, the follies and horrors of Passchendaele.

Nevertheless, the Second Coalition ended the war triumphantly in November 1918, after many perilous and critical hazards. In a sense, therefore, it might be said to have achieved the purpose for which it sought and received the authority of Parliament.

What then was to be done? The Parliament was more than eight years old. A Dissolution and a General Election could not be avoided. But on what basis? It seemed barely credible that we should all go back to the pre-war position, with the old disputes and the old slogans. The public could not be asked, like a new Rip van Winkle, to put out of their minds the lacerating experiences of four years of the most terrible war in history, or to avert their eyes from the tangle of post-war problems confronting them, in order to return to the old, half-forgotten issues which divided parties in what seemed, especially to the young, the distant, almost shadowy, past. It may be argued that Lloyd George could have tried to widen his appeal, by a reconciliation with Asquith and the official Liberals. But he would almost certainly have been rebuffed. Perhaps, had he known the overwhelming victory which awaited him at the poll, he might have succeeded in restraining the not unnatural demands for full reparation, whether by 'Hanging the Kaiser' or 'Making the Germans pay in full'. (The dreadful phrase 'squeeze them till the pips squeak' was not his own.) In any event, he and his colleagues were returned in November 1918 by a huge majority and, in one form or another, the Coalition lasted till the autumn of 1922.

The story of these years – 1918 to 1922 – illustrates one of the main difficulties involved in organising general consent at a time of crisis, especially if that crisis is prolonged. If sometimes the British public accepts coalitions with general acclaim at their start, it seems to get tired of them when they have lasted a certain time. This may be because the original impetus leading to the sinking of political and personal claims makes too heavy a demand on human nature to be sustained at a high moral level; or it may be because when the original object has been more or less attained the new combination seems to have no justifiable purpose and to be continuing its existence mainly for its own benefit.

Asquith's coalition which kept nearly all the power in the hands of himself and his Liberal colleagues and merely brought into prominence a few old parliamentary friends had little effect. It left the party system and the party loyalties unshaken and involved no very bitter partings. The chief loser was Churchill who was forced to sink from the position of First Lord of the Admiralty, in which he had shone supreme, into the comparative obscurity of the Duchy of Lancaster. Asquith's coalition as a whole made no heavy strain upon individuals or parties.

Lloyd George's War Government was very different. The most bitter feelings were created and remained over the next generation between the two leaders and their families and friends. Asquith, himself a man of great self-control and dignity, was supported or perhaps egged on by his wife and daughter who regarded him as having a more or less permanent claim to No. 10 Downing Street and as a victim of Lloyd George's cynical and sinister plots. Although Dame Margaret Lloyd George took little part in politics, Lloyd George and his daughter Megan were quite a match for the Asquiths. Unhappily nearly all the leading Liberal politicians remained loyal to Asquith. Able, complacent, self-satisfied and narrow, the McKennas, Runcimans, Samuels and the like became permanently estranged. The Liberal Party in the House of Commons was split into two almost equal groups. In 1916 it had been the dominant political power in Britain, with nearly three hundred Members to the House of Commons. By the election of 1918 the Coalition or Lloyd Georgian Liberals could muster over one hundred and thirty Members, while the official or Asquithian Liberal Party had been practically annihilated, only twenty-eight Members being elected throughout the country. This was the unhappy legacy of Lloyd George's great War Government; for it was one of the greatest Governments in our history. By projecting itself into the post-war period, it inevitably caused or at least facilitated almost a revolution in our political structure. The Liberal Party sank and has never recovered. There have been spasmodic revivals sufficient to win a considerable number of votes but very few seats. Nor has there been any clear philosophy, but rather a reliance upon those parts of the population that have temporarily lost faith in the other political parties. It has become, inevitably, a party of 'protest'. Whether without the Asquith–Lloyd George rivalry, without the break up of the old Liberal Party, the decline was inevitable, who can tell? Some might claim that the Labour Party was certain to take the place of the upper and middle class Liberals, an 'establishment' based on their academic distinctions or their great successes in business and at the bar; that these were bound to make way for the new Labour movement, just as the Whigs had ultimately to give way to the Liberals and Radicals.

The first Labour Members in the House of Commons were, of course, representative of what were then called the 'working classes'. Many of them had actually 'worked'. But as years passed all this began to change, and it may indeed be claimed that the true successors of the Liberal Party, as it existed before the First World War – a combination of moderates and extremists, Whigs, Liberals and Radicals, men of many walks of life, of rich and poor – are to be found in the new Labour Party which during recent years has been transformed and captured, or at any rate influenced, by the fortunate products of the public schools and of the universities old and new. By a strange paradox the moderate section is still largely composed of men of industrial experience. The more extreme position has been occupied by the intellectuals.

At any rate this transformation resulted not only from the war period but from the succeeding years between 1918 and 1922. When Lloyd George fell from a position of authority scarcely held by any Prime Minister in history; he fell never, in terms of political power, to rise again. The 1931 Coalition was somewhat different, for important reasons. Both Asquith's and Lloyd George's coalitions were based on the indisputable and evident demands and dangers of actual war. MacDonald's was formed to deal with the less obvious, or at least more disputable, prospect of bankruptcy. Moreover, while the Labour Party, after a close vote, decided not only to support but to participate in the Government of 1916, the mass of the party, following their party boss, Arthur

Henderson, not merely refused to join but became immediately and bitterly hostile to the new regime. MacDonald only carried with him a few individuals the most notable, of course, being Philip Snowden. The National Labour Party, as his supporters were called, only put forward twenty candidates at the General Election of 1931 of which thirteen were elected. The official Labour Party was able to field over five hundred candidates and elect fifty-two, polling 6,600,000 votes. Thus the Labour schism was incomparably less dramatic than the Liberal split in 1916 or even than the success which the Liberal Unionists had achieved under Lord Hartington and Joseph Chamberlain when with about seventy seats they contributed a vital force and a new energy to Conservatism. The National Labour Party in effect consisted of the Prime Minister, the Chancellor of the Exchequer, the Lord Chancellor, Mr J. H. Thomas, and their immediate followers. The rank and file contributed little or nothing. Moreover MacDonald's political philosophy and thought had stopped some years before. Snowden had never really developed beyond the position of a Cobdenite radical. Nevertheless the National Government in one form or another succeeded in its immediate task. Even in 1935 so great was the original impetus that it was able to retain power although it had now become almost purely a Conservative Administration. There were a few Liberal Nationals who contributed something significant, and one or two remaining National Labour. But in effect the Government had become, after MacDonald's resignation, a purely Conservative administration. It drifted on through the late thirties to its dramatic if somewhat inglorious end in May 1940.

The bitter memories of MacDonald's decision (some would say treachery) in 1931 have made any similar solution of a similar national emergency improbable. Yet it is by no means impossible. After all, whatever may be the conflicting views of historians as to the need for so drastic a decision in order to meet the immediate difficulties, it cannot be denied that the formation of the coalition, or National Government, brought the necessary confidence to overcome the pressing and urgent dangers. A nation apparently drifting to internal strife and external bankruptcy was in fact rescued by its own efforts, under the leadership of a group of statesmen which was brought into being honourably and for patriotic purposes. At any rate, when Hitler's invasion of Europe at last led to the end of the Chamberlain regime, the nation did not demand a return to party government. There was a universal cry for a true national government, representing a unified effort under the only man judged capable of maintaining what seemed at the time an almost hopeless struggle against the forces of evil.

I remember Churchill saying to me soon after the formation of the Government in 1940, 'I have formed the widest administration ever made in British politics. It ranges from Lord Lloyd to Miss Ellen Wilkinson – from Dolobran to Jarrow.' And so it proved. The nation faced with the dangers of 1940 universally demanded a national government, 'The Great Coalition', as Churchill named it on the medal which he sent in 1945 to every member of all the parties who had served in his administration.

But this Government, in spite of its glorious record was by general agreement brought to an end as soon as the war with Germany was over. Since 1945, in spite of many perplexing problems and acute dangers which Britain has had to face there has been no attempt to revive a national government. There has been much talk, but little action. But then, there has been no comparable crisis, even to that of 1931 – as yet.

II

Although except as a desperate remedy for desperate ills, national or coalition government is generally impracticable and unpopular, that is not to say that at all times, both in the narrow political world and outside, among what are called 'thinking men and women in all walks of life' there are not continual efforts to reach common agreement on common policies in order to make progress in the common good. One of such attempts reached notable proportions in the 1930s during the period of reconstruction follow-

ing the collapse of 1931 and before the whole scene was overcast
by the rise of the Hitler menace.

If I re-tell the story in some little detail, it is because I feel
that similar efforts, either in public or in private, may again have
great value in forming and guiding opinion against a day of
reckoning.

The parliamentary position in 1931 was almost without precedent. The Labour Party had been temporarily shattered, its
numbers reduced to just over fifty. The Liberal Party had been
broken into two sections. The Liberal Nationals closely allied with
the Conservatives had 35 Members; the official Liberals 33.
The total Conservative Members in the House of Commons was
473. Such a situation naturally led to a certain laxity both in
attendance and doctrine. With so huge a majority the division
lobby almost lost its importance. Yet the great Government army
consisted of many different forces temporarily welded together.
It was not therefore surprising that stresses began to appear. Only
with rare skill and determination was the Chief Whip, first Eyre-
Mansell, then David Margesson, able to keep together such a
diverse host.

When the official Liberals left the National Government on the
tariff issue it seemed that Liberalism was dooming itself to
obsolescence, for even many of the old Liberals recognised that
in the new conditions some tariff was necessary, partly for revenue
and partly for protective purposes. Free Trade, after all, had been
both the instrument and the result of fixed exchanges. With the
wild fluctuations now appearing in the exchange rates of different
countries, the old arguments seemed out of date.

Some of my friends and I made a substantial effort to secure
that the changes in fiscal policy should be accompanied by
industrial reconstruction and reorganisation. In a number of
speeches, articles and eventually booklets, of which the most
important was one called *Reconstruction*, I gathered round me a
team in my own party which included in particular north country
Members such as Cuthbert Headlam, Hugh Molson, Tom Martin
and Lord Eustace Percy. It is true that towards the end of Parlia-

ment we were deprived of Percy's experience for a time because he joined the Government as Minister without Portfolio. Happily, early in the next Parliament he resigned his office for the somewhat unusual reason that he had nothing to do. We soon gained adherents throughout the party. Although some of our old colleagues of the 1924 Parliament had been advanced or silenced by office, I set about creating a new group and within a year or two, with our speeches and pamphlets, we had become, if not a force, at least a recognisable body of opinion.

There now began a more interesting development. By the spring of 1935 fourteen Members of Parliament joined with me in the publication of a booklet called *Planning for Employment* which became the basis for a campaign carried on as energetically as we could throughout 1934 and 1935. Many others, in and outside Parliament, were sympathetic to the main theme, which was the need for a combination of industrial expansion and orderly planning – a true partnership between Government and industry, to replace the old *laissez-faire* structure now on the point of collapse. With the help of Henry Mond (the second Lord Melchett) I launched the Industrial Reorganisation League in the summer of 1934. Many Members of Parliament helped us as well as leading industrialists, such as Robert Horne, Felix Pole, former manager of the Great Western Railway, William Firth, a leading steel magnate, and Valentine Crittall. We also had the help of Lionel Hichens of Cammell Laird, Israel Sieff, one of the founders of Marks and Spencer, and many others. All this, which now seems so trite, was then almost revolutionary. But so far the new ideas had sprung almost entirely from the Conservative side. Yet I was convinced that there were many people of all parties and of none, who would support a line of approach which might give us both new hope in a period of deep confusion and spread a new spirit of co-operation in the nation.

Accordingly I was glad to attend a meeting in the summer of 1934 held at All Souls College, Oxford, under the chairmanship of the Warden. It was organised by a remarkable group and spread through a wide circle. Its leading spirit was Clifford Allen, now

Lord Allen of Hurtwood, one of the most intelligent men I have
known and one of the most attractive. He began life as an extreme
Left-Wing Socialist, a rebel and a conscientious objector. He was
later a leading member of the Independent Labour Party. Somewhat unexpectedly, in the great Labour schism, he threw in his
lot with Ramsay MacDonald. At the moment of crisis he wrote a
powerful article in favour of MacDonald's decision to form the
National Government. The *Daily Herald* refused it. It was
printed with considerable effect in the *Manchester Guardian*. It
was not unnatural that he should become chairman of the National
Labour Party, and at this point he accepted a peerage. In spite of
continuous ill-health, his energy and enthusiasm were unbounded
for any cause which he adopted. He seemed now to have gone
through a period of moral and intellectual enthusiasm amounting
to something like religious conversion. It was in this spirit that he
became the promoter of a movement which tried to substitute
reason and goodwill for bias and prejudice.

As a result of the meeting at Oxford it was proposed that a
book should be prepared, something in the nature of a manifesto.
The committee should be carefully chosen and balanced, and the
signatures of two or three hundred men and women of distinction
should be sought. Two drafting committees were formed, one on
home and one on foreign affairs. I joined the first, which met
sometimes in Oxford and sometimes in my house in London.
The most active amongst us were Geoffrey Crowther, Arthur Salter
and Hugh Molson. With men so busily employed in other occupations our work took some time, and it was not until July 1935 that
our volume, entitled *The Next Five Years* was published. On
economic policy it was an attempt to find a working compromise
between the extremes of collectivism and individualism, but it
was a compromise much to my taste. At the time it seemed to lean
rather more to the Left than to the Right, especially with regard
to the proposals for an increase in public or semi-public control of
utilities such as transport, gas and electricity. Today, however, it
would seem to be rather Right-Wing; so far have we travelled in
these years. But what were more novel were the policies for

industrial organisation including the participation of labour, for expansionist finance, and for the organisation of economic planning, both nationally and locally. This part of the book, to use today's jargon, might have been described as 'Left Centre'. What was remarkable, however, was not so much the precise proposals of *The Next Five Years* as the fact that they were made at all. Although the greater part of the signatories were not in politics as such, they included sixteen Members of Parliament, mostly supporters of the Government, including such 'respectable' figures as Major Jack Hills, Terence O'Connor and Geoffrey Ellis, former manager of Beckett's Bank. Among trade unionists were included John Bromley, then the secretary of A.S.L.E.F. and a former chairman of the T.U.C., Arthur Pugh, another former chairman of the T.U.C. and secretary of the Iron and Steel Trades Confederation. Of economists the most distinguished was, of course, Arthur Salter, one of the principal draftsmen. The Archbishop of York (Temple) and the Bishop of Birmingham (Barnes) represented the clergy. We also had as a signatory the great philosopher, S. Alexander, and such writers as Gilbert Murray, Desmond MacCarthy and H. G. Wells.

This movement marked a genuine attempt to bridge the gap between parties and interests, in a country that had just survived a serious crisis and was still in a depressed and even sullen mood. As the Election of 1935 approached, the work of our group became somewhat confused with Lloyd George's effort to come back into politics with his New Deal. Not unnaturally some of the members of Lord Allen's following were alarmed at the prospect of being charmed, fascinated and eventually absorbed by the Welsh wizard. Nevertheless the two movements continued and through the far-reaching connections of its signatories and supporters, no doubt some effect even upon the Government of the day.

I give this as an example of many similar efforts before and since to promote national movements within the existing political structure. Nevertheless I must confess that although they may have an important impact upon public opinion and therefore in the long run upon policy, they are rarely able to influence the great political machines which dominate and control parties. They can prepare the way for action; but they cannot set it in motion, even at a time of crisis.

III

To sum up: if the conditions are sufficiently desperate, war or economic collapse, the political structure in Britain has generally been flexible enough to meet the need. Coalitions or national governments and the like are somehow or other brought into being. They may be set up to meet a single need, and dissolve, as did the great coalition of 1940 to 1945, when the supreme purpose was achieved. They may continue in a different form as did the Governments of 1916 and 1931. Meanwhile as was proved throughout the nineteenth century and is again becoming apparent, any administration with even a nominal majority can, through a number of alliances and understandings, keep itself in being, oscillating sometimes to the Right, sometimes to the Left, making concessions here and there, offering bribes or menaces, and struggle through an apparent maze of difficulty without having any clear majority in the country and only a slender authority in the House of Commons. The Whigs achieved it with great success in the period between the first Reform Bill of 1832 and the second Reform Bill of 1867. Derby and Disraeli achieved it for short periods during their Administrations of 1858 to 1859 and 1866 to 1868 when their party was in a minority. Recent events show that with good manipulation the same success, at least in appearance, can be maintained.

Certainly a new situation now faces us, more similar to the hard fought struggles of former centuries – a struggle for sovereignty. Even a united government, with an overwhelming parliamentary majority, may prove impotent in face of the new interests which can, if they so wish, bring the whole country to a halt. There is much talk, in the Press and among many moderate people of all parties, about a possible 'collapse'. The enormous gap between expenditure and revenue as well as the unfavourable balance of trade, has made us dependent on borrowing, mostly foreign borrowing. This source, entirely outside our control or even our influence, may prove timid or volatile. Short-term borrowing can quickly come to an end, and funds so deposited can be withdrawn at a few days' notice. Moreover, if the inflation in Britain continues at a rate quite out of step with other European countries, confidence in Britain's future may first be weakened and then totally destroyed. It is in preparation for such a disaster that much preliminary thought should be given to the possible remedies, whether immediate or long-term. It seems more important that men and women of goodwill, including politicians and even leaders of parties, should devote some of their efforts to this constructive work, rather than continue to indulge in those contests of negative recrimination and abuse which have done so much to weary the public.

But we must not imagine that even if a new political or parliamentary coalition could be brought into existence, that the nation would have obtained more than the preliminary instrument essential to the task of reform and reconstruction. Great struggles, involving bitter and often dangerous crises, would have to be faced. The technical developments in the character of public services, such as power and transport; the changes in many industrial processes already described; above all, the infiltration of the executives of the trade unions by Communist or semi-Communist forces has weakened any government, however complete its support in Parliament, in facing these new and formidable forces of disruption. The contest may be long and painful. But desperate ills often require desperate remedies.

Epilogue

Old age and youth suffer in common from the difficulty of seeing events or individuals in their true perspective. To the young schoolboy the heads of the school and the leading figures in athletics or scholarship are heroes; the masters, especially the headmaster, seem prodigies of learning and command respect and even fear. They remain for ever in the nostalgic memory of early days as figures of supermen – semi-divine. Never again will there be boys or masters cast from such a mould. Their successors seem puny and hardly worthy of deference, still less of awe.

Similarly, old men treasure with special regard the great figures known only from a distance in earlier years. There will never again be statesmen or even politicians equal to those commanding figures of the past. There will be no rhetoric; nothing but turgid economic jargon. No fine debates in the House of Commons; nothing but petty squabbles. No exciting duels between giants; only squalid disputes between pygmies. The memories of the first years of this century recorded in these pages are necessarily subject to the same general rule. I see the men and women whom I have tried to describe through a haze of passing years. Naturally, therefore, I exaggerate the strength and value of those whom I saw as a child or as a growing man. Their successors I view in a different light, and tend no doubt to under-rate their qualities.

Nevertheless, in the political sphere at any rate, most of those I have described, partly because of the circumstances in which they worked, partly because of the greater respect paid to Parliament, partly because of the absence of competition from other organisations claiming public attention, had some outstanding quality, rarely evident today. Whether the present generation in fact equals or even surpasses the old it will fall to another to decide. Certainly the conditions in which these men had to work were different from those which confront their successors. Up to 1914 (the First World War) and even to a lesser extent up to 1939 (the Second World War), Britain and the mass of the people of Britain lived in an atmosphere of security which it is difficult fully to realise today. In the old balance of world power Britain and the British Empire stood almost at the apex of wealth and potential military strength. In the First War Britain and France succeeded in overcoming the forces of the German and Austro-Hungarian Empires even after the defection of Russia. The contribution of America was great in terms of money and supplies; in terms of fighting forces, almost negligible. In 1939 nations of the old Commonwealth stood firmly united with the old country, in spite of the independence which they won in the First War and which was fully recognised by the Statute of Westminster, the essential unity of the old Empire remaining unchallenged. This was proved when every independent dominion – Canada, Australia, South Africa and New Zealand – sprang immediately to the help of the mother country. The vast Indian Empire as well as all the Colonial territories in different parts of the world were similarly united. Thus the men and women whom I have tried to describe were conscious of being subjects of an almost unique imperial system, powerful and progressive as well as prosperous. Although they could not look to a home population equal in numbers or perhaps in wealth to those of the New World, yet they felt no sense of inferiority to any other nation or group of nations. Indeed they still gloried in the primacy which had followed one hundred years of that Pax Britannica to which all the world looked with respect, if not always with affection.

Conditions which we have had to face since the end of the Second War are wholly different. The countries of the old Commonwealth, still linked to Britain by affection and interest, have developed more and more their own life and are increasingly confronted with their own special problems. The Colonial Empire has been, by an irresistible process, accelerated if not created by the Second World War, developed into a number of independent nations, still happily within the Commonwealth. But after tearing itself apart for the second time within a generation by frightful and internecine struggles, lasting altogether ten years, the relative position of what remains of Europe is gravely reduced. Partitioned by what Churchill first called 'The Iron Curtain', the countries of free and democratic Europe are incomparably weaker in respect of the whole world than they were in the times of which I have tried to recall some of the leading figures and describe the atmosphere. Europeans, for more than two thousand years supreme in the world, are now, even though in part at last united, no greater in wealth, population or resources than America, Russia or China. If divided in foreign or defence policy their influence is still further reduced. At the same time, in spite – or perhaps because – of the rapid, even spectacular, social developments in this country, the decay of Parliament relative to the power of the trade unions seems to threaten the Parliamentary authority almost as menacingly as did the Medieval Church, the great Barons or the King in former struggles. The change or, as many would think, the decay of the old moral system which bound our people together; the loss of authority by the churches; the weaker ties of family life; a growth of scepticism, almost nihilism, among the young – all these have made the task of our statesmen today more difficult and more discouraging. Without any sense of security themselves they live in an insecure and changing world. Yet these troubles may be more apparent than real, more temporary than permanent. All through history there seemed to be periods of almost inevitable collapse. Revolution was as much foreseen in the years following Waterloo as in the years that have followed the Second World War. Moreover, the very difficulties with which we are confronted offer new opportunities. The future of Britain lies in the hands of her people and the leadership which is given by those who aspire to positions of authority. Science, technology, the enormous possibilities in the creation of wealth, the wide distribution of high living standards, the spread of knowledge, the opportunities of education on a scale which our forebears would not have believed – all these are available if the moral urge and the idealism to which our predecessors could appeal can be brought into play. Most of the wounds from which we suffer today are self-inflicted, and therefore lie within our own power to salve. Now that Britain has definitely taken her place in Europe there is an ever-widening scope for looking outwards rather than inwards, both to the nations of Europe and to the outer world. If the old Empire has gone, the vision of the new Commonwealth can be realised in the co-operation of the nations of the old Commonwealth with those of the new and developing nations. Britain, in Europe and in the Commonwealth, has surely a great part to play.

Yet the questions still haunt me – and others too. Is this a temporary setback, or the beginning of a slow decline? The old supremacy has gone, of course, and can never recur. Yet the contribution which Britain has made to civilisation has not depended only on her wealth and military or naval strength. We are apt to be too much obsessed by the nineteenth century and the almost effortless superiority which we then achieved. In former ages our population was small and our resources undeveloped; but our spirit was undefeatable – often heroic. Can there be now a new renaissance or must we reconcile ourselves to an inevitable, if gradual, ebbing of the tide? 'There is a lot of ruin,' said Adam Smith, 'in a great nation.' So the selfish or the cynical may comfort themselves with the reflection that it should, with luck, last their time.

For myself, I have more confidence – if you like, faith. It is a dangerous thing to say about the British people that they are finished – that they 'have had it' in the slang of today. They have a remarkable power of recovery once they are determined and united.

Here comes again the old question. How do the politicians (or statesmen) of today compare with those of the past? How would the men of whom I have tried to draw a sketch have dealt with the problems with which we are now faced? Is there, in reality, little difference in the men? The usual hesitations, procrastinations, compromises, party prejudices, refusal to face reality until almost overwhelmed by disaster – have I not told the melancholy story, at any rate in respect of the inter-war years? Are we not now, as then, waiting for leadership? If we had it, should we reject it, as Lloyd George and Churchill were discarded in the locust years?

Yet this is too harsh a judgment, perhaps, both on the past and the present men and women who have entered public life, for many different, but on the whole honourable, motives. After all, politics is the 'art of the possible'. In a parliamentary, and still more in a democratic, system it is no use trying to achieve what is palpably impossible – at least under the conditions of the moment. We must persuade, we cannot compel. In this delicate balance, timing is all important. Of course, the general ought to lead his army; but he must not be too far ahead. Indeed, in modern warfare he must usually be behind.

All this is true. It was the guiding principle of the Walpoles, the Newcastles, and many others under whom Britain has often prospered, down to the Asquiths and the Baldwins. It was not that of the Chathams, the Pitts, down to the Lloyd Georges and Churchills, under whom Britain has been succoured and raised to heights of imperishable glory. But this is only to say that extraordinary times need extraordinary men. We can jog along all right (and perhaps more comfortably) in what used to be called 'normal' times with men of lesser stature, who do good service in their own way.

Finally, what brings men into politics – whether men of genius or more humble endowments? Certainly a desire to serve and even shine in an honourable profession. For some, it is enough merely to serve, loyally and humbly. For others, to reach moderate, respectable and useful positions of influence and authority. For a few, who despise money, or outward honours, or even the plaudits of the crowd – the everlasting lure is power.

All these, in their different ways, are engaged in 'the Endless Adventure' of governing men. I have tried to recall some memories of a few of these men in the years from 1906 to 1939. For those who have had to steer on the perilous and stormy seas in which the world has been engulfed since that fearful catastrophe – the Second World War – we can feel at least sympathy, if not always admiration.

Notes and Acknowledgements

In this book I have touched upon a few topics and incidents already described in *Winds of Change*, and in so doing have used much the same words as before. These passages are indicated in the notes relating to the individual chapters, together with other works which have been helpful in writing this book. C. L. Mowat's *Britain Between the Wars* (1968) and *British Political Facts, 1900–1968* (1969) by David Butler and Jennie Freeman have been consulted throughout.

CHAPTER ONE: *An Honourable Ambition*
Thomas Hughes's *Memoir of Daniel Macmillan* (1882) quotes the passages from my grandfather's letter on pages 12–13, which are also used in *Winds of Change*. Morley's description of Alexander Macmillan on page 22 comes from his *Recollections* (1917).

CHAPTER TWO: *Lloyd George*
Frank Owen's *Tempestuous Journey: Lloyd George, His Life and Times* (1954) has been useful throughout this chapter. Keynes's account of the end of the blockade and Lloyd George's part in getting food supplies to Germany referred to on page 48 is told in 'Dr Melchior' in *Two Memoirs* (1949). Much of the paragraph on page 70 concerning the relations between The Next Five Years Group and Lloyd George appeared in *Winds of Change*, as did the account of Lloyd George's speech of 18 June 1936, here printed on pages 72–4. Lloyd George's letter, mentioned on page 76, refusing Churchill's offer of a place in the War Cabinet is quoted in A. J. Sylvester's *Life with Lloyd George* (1975).

CHAPTER THREE: *Ramsay MacDonald*
Lloyd George's remarks on page 87 are quoted in *Tempestuous Journey*. A version of the paragraph on the Zinoviev letter on page 88 appeared in *Winds of Change*.

CHAPTER FOUR: *The National Government*
The quotations from C. L. Mowat on page 105 are from his book *Britain Between the Wars, 1918–1940* (1968).

CHAPTER FIVE: *Stanley Baldwin*
The instances of Baldwin's oratory quoted on page 124 are taken from G. M. Young's *Stanley Baldwin* (1952); the quotation from Middlemas and Barnes on page 119 is from their *Baldwin* (1969).

CHAPTER SIX: *Neville Chamberlain*
Iain Macleod's *Neville Chamberlain* (1961) has been useful throughout and has been quoted on pages 126, 134 and 138. Hoare's account of 'The Big Four' on page 136 is in his *Nine Troubled Years* (1954) written after he became Viscount Templewood.

CHAPTER SEVEN: *Churchill*
The quotations from Churchill's letters of January 1928 on page 157 also appear in *Winds of Change*, as did my account on pages 163–4 of my visit to Chartwell in April 1939. The diary quotation on page 166 is from Macleod's *Neville Chamberlain*.

CHAPTER TEN: *Independent Members*
The description of Maxton on page 204 follows that in *Winds of Change*.

I should also like to thank Lord Blake for his kindness in reading and commenting on the book in manuscript.

H.M.